A Son is Given

A Son is Given

Christ in Isaiah

Harry Uprichard

 EVANGELICAL PRESS

EVANGELICAL PRESS
12 Wooler Street, Darlington, Co. Durham, DL1 1RQ, England

© Evangelical Press 1992
First published 1992

British Library Cataloguing Publication Data available

ISBN 0 85234 301 9

Printed and bound in Great Britain at the Bath Press, Avon

To Maisie

Contents

Acknowledgements

Grateful thanks are expressed to all who have helped in this work, to Mrs Daniel McKee for her assiduous attention in typing the manuscript, to my friends and colleagues Rev. J. L. Heaney and Rev. N.W. McAuley for advice and proofreading, to the staff of Evangelical Press for undertaking the venture and to my wife Maisie for all her patience and encouragement in writing.

Harry Uprichard
Trinity Manse, Ahoghill,
November 1992

Preface

The inspiration of finding Christ in Isaiah springs from the fact that Christ is evident in all Scripture. It is an exciting quest too. The two travellers on the Emmaus road discovered that for themselves. Dejected and dispirited, feeling that all hopes of Israel's restoration were finally dashed to pieces, they found their hearts burning within them as the stranger walked and talked with them. But what was most important of all was the source to which they attributed those feelings. It was as Christ opened the Scriptures to them that this happened. Luke is quite specific in his description of Jesus' teaching on that occasion: 'Beginning with Moses and all the Prophets, [Christ] explained to them what was said in all the Scriptures concerning himself' (Luke 24:27).

Later, when Jesus appeared to the disciples in Jerusalem, this was again the precise nature of his instruction. 'He said to them, "This is what I told you while I was still with you: Everything must be fulfilled that is written about me in the Law of Moses, the Prophets and the Psalms." Then he opened their minds so they could understand the Scriptures' (Luke 24:44-45). Jesus used the three traditional divisions of the Old Testament — the Law, the Prophets and the Writings, for the Psalms is the first book of that last section — to emphasize the breadth of his message. He was claiming that everything in the entire Old Testament found its fulfilment in himself. As Christ, he was the one of whom substantially the Scriptures spoke. He was their central message, their primary subject matter. All the varied records, the wanderings of the patriarchs, the history of the kings, the oracles of the prophets, the psalms and proverbs of the wise men — all were about him. Christ is the story-line of Scripture. Augustine put it strikingly when he said, 'The New is in the Old concealed; the Old is in the New revealed.'

All Scripture is about Christ, both Old and New Testaments. That is what makes the Bible so exciting. That is what gives it cohesion. It is not simply that Christ is in the Scriptures. The Scriptures are primarily and fundamentally about Christ. The thrill of this emerges in each part of the Old Testament in its own particular way. The Law finds paradoxically both its completion and abolition in Christ. The foresight of the Prophets eventually reaches its climax in the coming of the Messiah. The wisdom of the Writings is personalized in Jesus, the living Word.

The prophets present this disclosure intriguingly. As, in God's name, they foretell the future, there is both immediate and ultimate fulfilment. Their words had significance for the age in which they lived. By the fulfilment of their oracles in the history of their day, they were adjudged either true or false prophets. But their words had a deeper import. Ultimately, they pointed forward to the coming of the Messiah, God's anointed Deliverer. That was what their message was really about. Immediate, even intervening, fulfilment was only the shadow of which Christ was the reality. Jesus explained this, among other things, to the disciples on the Emmaus road and at Jerusalem. That excited and reinvigorated them and made their hearts burn within them.

As Christ is in all the prophets, so Christ is in all Isaiah, not just in the purple passages. Christ is the substance of all Isaiah's prophecies, interwoven into the fabric of the historical context. On one level, we see Isaiah in his own lifetime warning a fearful Ahaz to rely on God alone and not on a Syrian/Israelite coalition against the advancing Assyrians, or restraining an over-zealous Hezekiah from anti-Assyrian intrigue. But the real message is in the Child Deliverer, the Branch from the house of David, through whom God would break Assyrian power, an ultimate promise of great David's greater Son. The judgements of God through the prophet against the surrounding nations and, indeed, against Israel and Judah in the earlier part of the prophecy, are simply an accompaniment to this theme.

At another point, Isaiah addressed a situation some two hundred years later when the Jews were in exile in Babylon. Foretelling God's purposes through future events, the prophet predicted the remarkable deliverance from Babylonian captivity through the Persian king, Cyrus, when the Persians eventually broke the power of Babylon and permitted the Jews to return to their homeland and rebuild the temple. So Isaiah describes Cyrus as God's anointed, a messiah. The welter of encouragements Isaiah brings to God's people in the latter part of his prophecy simply flesh out this glad news of deliverance. Again, the essential message lies deeper. The ultimate fulfilment of Isaiah's words of comfort and hope does not end with the return from Babylon. They are completed in the coming of the true Messiah, Jesus. He is the eternal agent of God's comfort to his people, the Suffering Servant who dies for his people, the Deliverer who leads them to drink of gospel waters without money and without price. Again, Christ is the theme — not just Christ *in* Isaiah but Christ *throughout* Isaiah. The whole prophecy is ultimately about Jesus.

This is the theme of the following pages. But to trace out that design we shall concentrate on some of the purple passages, not because Christ is evident only in these, but because he is supremely evident in them. This overview will set the parameters of the prophet's essential message. Immediate and ultimate fulfilment will fuse excitingly together. What was predicted hundreds of years before of Jesus' birth will be realized in Jesus' life, teaching, death and resurrection. In that sense, the Old will be revealed in the New.

When, as Luke records in Acts, the Ethiopian treasurer was reading in his chariot from Isaiah 53 he was confused (Acts 8:26-40). To whom was the prophet referring when he spoke of the sufferings of the Servant, to himself or to someone else? Philip began with that passage of Scripture and told him the good news about Jesus. The change in the treasurer was dramatic. He was no longer confused; he was excited — excited to the point of repentance and faith, excited enough to desire baptism. His understanding of the Christ of Isaiah led him to faith in Jesus. The burning hearts of the two on the Emmaus road, the realization of the disciples who listened to Jesus opening the Scriptures to them and the perception of the treasurer's faith are all of a piece. If our study of Christ in Isaiah even minimally warms our hearts, clears the confusion, directs our understanding, leads to faith and growth in the Saviour and glorifies Jesus, it will more than repay any effort made in writing it.

1.
The coming of Christ

The year was 735 B.C. The stable reign of King Uzziah had passed and difficulties loomed large on Judah's borders. The kings of Aram and Israel combined forces and threatened Jerusalem, and the people of Judah were obsessed by this danger. Uzziah's death some years previously had been the occasion when God had called Isaiah as a prophet (Isa. 6:1). The message which God commanded him to proclaim was one of God's holiness and his judgement on the nation because of sin. Within that message, however, was an element of hope. Judah looked to Isaiah for help from God in such days of tension and unrest.

In these circumstances, the prophet Isaiah brought a word from God (Isa. 7:1-17). The gist of the message was that Judah was worrying about the wrong enemy. Rezin, King of Aram, and Pekah, son of Remaliah, King of Israel, were 'two smouldering stubs of firewood' who would soon be extinguished. Indeed, a child would be born, and before he reached the years of understanding, these two dreaded kings would be destroyed. The child's name was to be 'Immanuel', meaning 'God with us'. That, in itself, was significant. It meant that God would be with them whatever troubles they faced.

The real enemy lay further north, Isaiah claimed. It was the growing power of the Assyrian empire. However, Judah must fear God, not man. While God would use Assyria to discipline Judah, eventually God's people would be delivered from this greater threat. Even the power and might of Assyria would not frustrate God's promise to David and to his heirs. God's covenant with his people was firm and sure. That covenant was a solemn promise of God to his people going back to Abraham. God promised that he would bless and care for his people like a father. It was a covenant based on God's sovereign choice and divine initiative.

Isaiah brought another message from God. It gave further encouragement to Judah in these tense circumstances. Like many of his prophecies, it spoke not only to the immediate situation, but ultimately of God's promise of a Messiah. The details are striking. We find them in Isaiah 9:1-7. This is one of the passages often read at Christmas, for it is a prophecy of the coming of Christ. While this prophecy was in part fulfilled in Isaiah's day, it points forward to the eventual birth of the Messiah. In that sense, it takes up the story of the earlier promise of 'Immanuel'. As we pursue the message of Isaiah 9:1-7, it presents an impressive picture of the coming of Christ. We understand more clearly why Isaiah has sometimes been called 'the evangelist of the Old Testament'.

Light from darkness

Isaiah's word concentrated on the birth of a child. The details point clearly to the coming of Christ. The birth of this child will bring light into a situation of darkness. The gloom of turmoil and confusion will be penetrated by the clarity of order and purpose. Fear will give way to calm. Distress and hunger will be replaced by ease and satisfaction. The Messiah's coming will be like dawn skirting across the dark landscape and bathing everything in bright sunlight.

The place

The place of the occurrence is important: 'Nevertheless, there will be no more gloom for those who were in distress. In the past he humbled the land of Zebulun and the land of Naphtali, but in the future he will honour Galilee of the Gentiles, by the way of the sea, along the Jordan—

> The people walking in darkness
>   have seen a great light;
> on those living in the land of the shadow of death
>   a light has dawned'

(Isa. 9:1-2).

The location is precise. Zebulun and Naphtali were the tribal areas immediately to the west of the Sea of Galilee. These areas were the first to suffer from Assyrian attack. Of course, throughout its history the whole land of Canaan experienced the gloom of foreign invasion. The iron chariots of the Midianites, the sweeping hordes of Philistines, the snorting stallions of Assyria, the incursions successively of Babylonian, Greek and Roman armies — all contributed to the continuing supremacy of foreign powers over their little territory. Here was the promise of brighter days ahead and, pointedly, in this particular area around Galilee. Even in Jesus' day, however, Galilee was regarded as a despised district from which no prophet was ever expected to come (John 7:52).

Matthew, in his Gospel, quotes this passage from Isaiah (Matt. 4:15-16). He mentions that Jesus left Nazareth, his home village, and went and lived in Capernaum, on the lakeside of Galilee in the area of Zebulun and Naphtali, specifically to fulfil this prophecy. Matthew regarded Jesus' movements in this district as noteworthy. What Jesus did during his ministry in Galilee confirms the significance of Isaiah's words and Matthew's interpretation of them. Jesus read from the scroll of Isaiah in his home village of Nazareth and referred this scripture to himself. He stilled the raging waves on Galilee and walked on its surface. He raised from death a widow's son at Nain, ten miles away, and turned water into wine at Cana of Galilee. In a practical way, from the very outset of Jesus' ministry, dawn had broken upon the region of Zebulun and Naphtali and the darkness of sickness and sin was fading away.

The time

The time of this fulfilment was also significant. Matthew notes that it was when Jesus heard that John had been put in prison that he returned to Galilee and then made his way to Capernaum. Matthew also points out that it was from that time on that Jesus began to preach, 'Repent, for the kingdom of heaven is near' (Matt. 4:17; cf. Mark 1:14-15).

Jesus did this intentionally. It was as though John the Baptist's imprisonment marked the time for Jesus' ministry proper to begin. It was the signal for him to move to Capernaum. Jesus continued and completed the work started by John. His message was substantially the same as John's. John was the promised forerunner, Jesus the promised Messiah. As the forerunner started his mission in the Desert of Judea, the Messiah got his under way in the district of Galilee. The two were not only linked in terms of location, but also related in terms of time.

Light penetrates darkness

The place and time were both right. The light penetrated the darkness. But that is not all. Equally important is the way Isaiah's prophecy motivated both John and Jesus. John's dress, message and the location of his ministry also recalled Isaiah's prophecy. Jesus' movements, timing and his words in the synagogue in Nazareth all pointed in the same direction. Both the coming of John and Jesus had their roots in the prophecy of Isaiah in terms of place and time.

The idea of light penetrating darkness marked Christ's ministry. The light continued to shine in the darkness and the darkness could not overpower it. John the Baptist was a lamp truly reflecting God's greatness. Jesus, however, was the uncreated light, the ultimate source of light. Jesus claimed that he was the light of the world. Those who followed him would not walk in darkness but have the light of life. The problem with those who rejected him was that they insisted they could see when, in fact, they were blind. God, who created light, had made light to shine in hearts, giving the light of the knowledge of his glory in the face of Christ.

Darkness causes confusion and disorder. I remember learning that forcefully on one occasion. It was the first Sunday of a new year and I was hurrying home to attend an evening communion service. A tree had fallen outside the manse. When I got indoors all was in darkness. I rushed and stumbled in the darkness preparing to go to church. When I arrived, the church building was perfectly lighted and I had time to check my notes and regain my calm. The light brought order and purpose out of chaos and confusion. I thought about that as I drove home. Christ, the light of the world, penetrates the confusion and disorder caused by sin in our lives. He pours 'celestial light' on the eyeballs of the blind. He brings calm, order and purpose to lives shattered and confused by sin.

It is for this reason that Christians are a community of light in which the sinful works of darkness have no rightful place. God has shone into believers' hearts the knowledge of Christ the light. God has called them out of darkness into his marvellous light through Christ. It is because God is light, and in him is no darkness at all, that Christians can walk in the light. They do this through Jesus, God's Son, who purifies them from all sin.

Christians, then, are the light of the world. Their good works are to be seen, not hidden, but seen in such a way as to glorify God, not self. As Christians, we have been brought from the darkness of sin into God's marvellous light. Our daily living must reflect the character of God who called us. We are the sons of the day, not of the night. Alertness and self-control, not drunkenness and confusion, should mark our activities. We are children of light, not of darkness. The fruit of light, which is goodness, righteousness and truth, should be evident in us. We must expose the fruitless deeds of darkness.

The Christ of Isaiah comes to dispel darkness with light. He comes to the proper place and at the right time to fulfil God's promises to his people. The relevance of Christ is that he both reveals and destroys the darkness of sin. This thought of the relevance of Christ should not escape us. Isaiah stresses it as he introduces his prophecy.

The New Testament takes up the theme. It was when the time was ripe that God sent his Son. Christ came to his own place but his own people did not accept him. Christ is the total fulfilment, the 'yes' and 'Amen', of all God's promises. The Christ, who scatters the gloom and darkness of sin from men's hearts, does so at just the right time and in exactly the correct way. Christ is the answer to every need and he meets us precisely at the point of our need. Christ does not speak unclearly or work superficially. He pinpoints the source of darkness and leads to the light to be found only in himself.

Isaiah later describes the Messiah as a 'light for the nations'. Here, at the very outset, Christ is portrayed as a light for Judah. The final measure ultimately of Christ's victory is evident in a church comprised of both Jews and Gentiles marked by light in their character, activities and lifestyle. But the dawn had come and the darkness of night was scattered. Isaiah's long-awaited prophecy was being fulfilled. Morning had broken.

Liberation from slavery

The Christ of Isaiah comes to bring release to those in slavery. When the light has dawned, Isaiah promises prosperity in Judah. An enlarged nation will be a prospect of great joy. It will be like a plentiful harvest or the spoils of victory. We note how Isaiah uses a past tense to denote a future event, so certain is he that God's promises will be fulfilled:

'You have enlarged the nation
    and increased their joy;
they rejoice before you
    as people rejoice at the harvest,
as men rejoice
    when dividing the plunder'

(Isa. 9:3).

Things were very different from that in Isaiah's day. The scorched earth around Galilee and the threat of devastation further south were constant reminders of impending disaster. These promises called to mind God's covenant with his people. As far back as Abraham, God had said that they would be a great nation. They would have their own land.

God would bless them and curse their enemies. God would be their God. Had God abandoned his covenant? The glorious days of Uzziah were over, the prosperous years of David and Solomon a dream of the past. They were a small, divided and oppressed nation living under the constant threat of invasion and even extinction. Isaiah's grand words would only serve to highlight this. Isaiah reminded them of the past, however, to give them hope for the future.

'For as in the day of Midian's defeat,
    you have shattered
the yoke that burdens them,
    the bar across their shoulders,
    the rod of their oppressor.
Every warrior's boot used in battle
    and every garment rolled in blood
will be destined for burning,
    will be fuel for the fire'

(Isa. 9:4-5).

The rule of Midian

The key to understanding Isaiah's message lay in his reference to 'the day of Midian's defeat'. They must go beyond Uzziah, Solomon and David, back to the time of Gideon to find a solution to their problem. The misery of those times was as great, if not greater, than their own. There had been many aspects to that misery. The details of the story are found in Judges chapters 6 and 7.

Danger was imminent. It challenged the covenant promises of God. Their status as a people was imperilled. The Midianites were like swarms of locusts which could not be counted. Possession of their land was threatened. The enemy camped on their territory and ruined their crops. The curse of defeat and subjugation surrounded them. Those days were so oppressive that they fled to caves and strongholds in the mountains. All God had promised them seemed to be lost.

Fear gripped the entire nation. Gideon's activities illustrated that. He threshed wheat in a winepress. Dreading that the Midianites would come and rob his family of what little grain was left after their repeated invasions, Gideon was afraid to use the threshing-floor. He threshed in the narrow hollowed rock they used for treading the grapes. At least there the crop was safer.

Idolatry was the order of the day. That was why God had allowed the Midianites to subdue Israel for seven years. Jehovah's exclusive lordship had been threatened. Altars of Baal, the local fertility god, and poles in honour of Asherah, Baal's female counterpart, littered the Israelite countryside. Jehovah, they thought, was the God of the hills. It was good to have the favour of Baal as well, now that they were a settled rather than a nomadic community. The first commandment was forgotten and God punished them with Midianite supremacy.

Doubts as to God's love arose. When Israel cried to God in their oppression, God sent a prophet, whose name is not given, to remind them of their escape from Egypt and to warn them against idolatry. But even when 'the angel of the Lord' assured Gideon that God was with him, Gideon questioned this. Where were all God's wonders recounted by their fathers, when God brought them out of Egypt? 'The Lord has abandoned us and put us into the hand of Midian,' he said.

The misery which sin causes

Isaiah recalled Midian's day to remind God's people of the abject misery from which God had delivered them. God, who shattered the yoke that burdened them, the bar across their shoulders, the rod of their oppressor in Midian's day, would do the same for his people facing Assyrian supremacy.

Christ, in proclaiming his kingdom, stressed the misery into which sin brings people. He warned of sin's dangers. Whoever commits sin is a slave to sin. He spoke fearfully of sin's results. We are not to fear those who destroy the body, but him who casts both body and soul into hell. He challenged the compromise of idolatry. A man cannot serve two masters, God and Mammon. He recognized the doubts which sin brings. His followers were not to worry about food, clothing or the future but to trust in God their heavenly Father. Christ taught his greatest lesson on sin's misery by dying to save his people from it. Only through Christ can they escape sin's ultimate misery of eternal death.

The *Larger Catechism,* written by the Reformers in the seventeenth century, gives a vivid description of the misery which sin causes: 'The fall brought upon mankind the loss of communion with God, his displeasure and curse; so as we are by nature children of wrath, bond-slaves to Satan, and justly liable to all punishments in this world and that which is to come' (*Larger Catechism,* 27).

We need to relearn the lesson of the misery which sin produces. While people fail to recognize the oppressive and fatal nature of sin's slavery, they cannot see the need for Christ's death. What Christ did on the cross remains the dying act of a good man, not the atoning action of the God-man. The cross, on these terms, provides example but no redemption. There is nothing from which to gain release. Midian's day, with its misery, danger, fear, idolatry and doubt, sets the scene of battle for Isaiah's Christ. Without that background, the battle is meaningless, the Christ no victor and Christ's coming irrelevant.

The miraculous power of God

Isaiah's allusion to Midian's evil day not only emphasizes the misery of man's sinful condition; it focuses on the miraculous power of God relieving man from his distress:

> 'You have shattered
>   the yoke that burdens them,
>   the bar across their shoulders,
>   the rod of their oppressor'
>
> (Isa. 9:4).

The deliverance was the work of God's sovereign power from start to finish. In it, Gideon was primarily responsive rather than taking the initiative. It began with Gideon's repentance. Gideon had not only been fearful; he had been faithless. He questioned the reality of God's promises and doubted God's intention to intervene on Israel's behalf. What a shock it must have been when the angel of the Lord required him to kill his father's bull, to desecrate the altar of Baal and destroy the Asherah pole, and all this in the name of Jehovah, whom Gideon doubted.

Obeying the angel involved a complete change of heart for Gideon. He naturally baulked at the prospect. He probably had ready-made excuses. In principle, he would be disobeying his father's authority. In practice, he would be risking his father's anger. The consequences of such an action were simply unthinkable. But Gideon did as the angel required. He obeyed God rather than man. The result was remarkable. His father Joash, instead of disciplining Gideon, left that process to Baal, if he had either the power or desire to do it. Gideon's repentance had won his father also.

What an example of true repentance Gideon is! Often, when people think of repentance, they think merely of feeling sorry for sin, but repentance goes far beyond feelings. True repentance involves a change of heart, a complete about-turn of life. Gideon not only felt sorry about his lack of faith; he turned from it and obeyed God. He turned right round and moved in the opposite direction. He started to trust God.

In this, too, he was totally responsive. He responded positively to the angel's message. But for the angel's message, Gideon would have continued threshing wheat in the winepress.

'Repentance unto life is a saving grace, whereby a sinner, out of a true sense of his sin, and apprehension of the mercy of God in Christ, doth, with grief and hatred of his sin, turn from it unto God, with full purpose of, and endeavour after, new obedience' (*Shorter Catechism,* 87).

The rest of the story continues the miraculous theme. Amassing an army of 32,000 troops, Gideon prepared to fight against the Midianites. God, however, had other plans. Having taught Gideon what repentance meant, God now taught him what faith involved. God whittled down Gideon's army to 300, by first discarding those who were fearful and then those who were careless. To crown it all, God gave Gideon victory over the Midianites by a trick that could hardly be called a military strategy. They smashed the jars, shouted their cry, 'A sword for the Lord and for Gideon!' and watched the Midianites running about in confusion. God proved to Gideon that the battle was not Gideon's but God's.

Faith is like that. It is total reliance on God. We come to God, in the first instance, as we repent of sin and trust Christ for forgiveness, and then God continues to lead us in that way of absolute dependence on him. Repentance started Gideon off on the road of faith, but his faith had to be developed and matured. Our faith needs the same. God increasingly shows us our need of him by making us totally dependent on him. We are confronted with obstacles in the Christian life and often pushed to breaking-point by sickness, bereavement, adversity and disappointment. Humanly speaking this seems ridiculous. It is as though God was destroying faith. He is not. He is shaping faith, moulding us to an even greater dependence on him. God is proving to us, in a miraculous way, that man's extremity becomes God's opportunity. God is showing his mighty power to save and to keep on saving his people.

In all of this, both repentance and faith, Gideon was largely a passive instrument. His obedience was required, his actions were involved, but the keynote of the episode was clearly God's activity. In recalling Midian's evil day, Isaiah is making precisely this point. By an act of sovereign, miraculous power in which man's place is minimal, God 'shattered the yoke that burdened them'. God accomplished a decisive victory and established a lasting peace.

The defeat of Assyria

Isaiah's prophecy may also have pointed forward to the defeat of the Assyrian army who, some time later, under the leadership of Sennacherib, threatened Jerusalem during the reign of Hezekiah. If this was so, the parallel is striking. For Sennacherib's army was destroyed in one night by the angel of the Lord, without Judah having to lift a sword. Lord Byron in his poem 'The Destruction of Sennacherib' recalls the scene:

> The Assyrian came down like the wolf on the fold,
> And his cohorts were gleaming in purple and gold;
> And the sheen of their spears was like stars on the sea,
> When the blue wave rolls nightly on deep Galilee.
>
> Like the leaves of the forest when Summer is green,
> That host with their banners at sunset were seen;
> Like the leaves of the forest when Autumn hath blown,
> That host on the morrow lay wither'd and strown.
>
> For the Angel of Death spread his wings on the blast,
> And breathed in the face of the foe as he pass'd;
> And the eyes of the sleepers wax'd deadly and chill,
> And their hearts but once heaved, and for ever grew still!
>
> And the widows of Asshur are loud in their wail,
> And the idols are broke in the temple of Baal;
> And the might of the Gentile, unsmote by the sword,
> Hath melted like snow in the glance of the Lord!

Christ is the deliverer promised by Isaiah

Our interest, however, does not lie mainly with Hezekiah and Sennacherib, but with Christ. Isaiah's Christ shatters the bondage and relieves the misery caused by sin. As God in Midian's day and in Assyria's day removed his people's oppression, so God, through Christ, broke the ultimate yoke of man's slavery to sin. God's accomplishment in destroying Midian and Assyria and the salvation he brought in Christ are all equally acts of God's sovereign power.

This theme runs through Christ's ministry and can be traced back to Isaiah in Christ's thinking. From the very outset Jesus perceived his ministry as releasing slaves from their bondage. He went to his home synagogue in Nazareth and read these words from Isaiah:

> 'The Spirit of the Lord is on me,
>   because he has anointed me
>   to preach good news to the poor.
> He has sent me to proclaim freedom for the prisoners

and recovery of sight for the blind,
to release the oppressed,
to proclaim the year of the Lord's favour'

(Luke 4:18-19; cf. Isa. 61:1-2).

Jesus' awareness of his role as Isaiah's liberator is clear from what he said after reading the scroll: 'Today this scripture is fulfilled in your hearing' (Luke 4:21). He regarded himself as the one who fulfilled Isaiah's prophecy.

As Jesus continued his ministry, he confirmed his Messianic work in the same way. He responded to John the Baptist's question from prison, 'Are you the one who was to come, or should we expect someone else?' (Matt. 11:3), like this: 'Go back and report to John what you hear and see: The blind receive sight, the lame walk, those who have leprosy are cured, the deaf hear, the dead are raised, and the good news is preached to the poor' (Matt. 11:4-5). These words recall Isaiah 35:5-6 and 61:1. As John thought over this reply and remembered how Jesus had left Nazareth to preach in Galilee, he would be sure that Jesus was the Christ, Isaiah's Christ.

Jesus showed his disciples his power over Satan and his ability to free people from sin. He confronted his enemies, the Jewish leaders, with their need of his liberating power. At the very close of his ministry, he stressed his authority even to Pilate. Isaiah's Christ remained in control to the very end.

In all of this, the sovereignty of the liberator's power is evident. Christ alone is the source of the authority which he had received from his Father and which, in part, he delegated to his friends. Those who experience his liberating power do so obediently and receptively. Then they are truly free. Christ miraculously liberates them from a miserable slavery over which they have no control. The source of this goes back to that reading from Isaiah in the synagogue at Nazareth and to the Christ, who in Midian's evil day, 'shattered the yoke that burdens them, the bar across their shoulders, the rod of their oppressor' (Isa. 9:4).

The Christ we proclaim must be the Christ of Isaiah. He does not come simply to give a helping hand and comfort in life's distresses. He comes as a powerful liberator to break the stranglehold of sin in our lives. The image of Christ that has been proclaimed has too often been of a weak and pathetic fellow-sufferer, whose function is to assist, not to liberate, an adviser too polite to be effective. This is far removed from Isaiah's Christ and from Jesus' own views of himself as liberator. We need to present a Christ victorious over sin and triumphant in daily living.

The Christ we worship and serve must be the Christ of Isaiah too. Our lives, set free from sin by his redemptive power, should not be compromised by materialism, nor cramped by legalism, nor marred by unrighteousness. If we are truly free, that liberty should mark our character and lifestyle in an expanding growth, which disdains the very thought of enslavement to the old nature and embraces the new with continued enthusiasm.

> Oh for a thousand tongues to sing
> My great Redeemer's praise,
> The glories of my God and King,
> The triumphs of his grace!
>
> He breaks the power of cancelled sin,
> He sets the prisoner free;
> His blood can make the foulest clean,
> His blood availed for me.

(Charles Wesley)

Order from chaos

When Isaiah spoke of a Christ who would penetrate the darkness with light and liberate an enslaved nation, it gave comfort to the people. What really brought them to the pinnacle of excitement, however, was the mention again of the birth of a child:

> 'For to us a child is born,
>   to us a son is given,
>   and the government will be on his shoulders'

(Isa. 9:6).

Isaiah had already prophesied the birth of a child called Immanuel, 'God with us' (Isa. 7:14). This was the token that the threat of Israel's and Aram's confederacy against Judah would be short-lived. Homer Hailey contrasts the prophecy of Isaiah 7:14 with Isaiah 9:6 in this way: 'There He was a sign given by the Lord; here He is a Ruler who brings salvation and deliverance to his people.' The former was a Messianic sign; the latter detailed the person and work of the Messiah. Anticipation would have mounted in Judah with that realization.

The humanity of the Messiah

The details of Isaiah's words were personal, human and divine. What could be more human than the birth of a child? They would perhaps have preferred a grown warrior. Circumstances being what they were, however, beggars could not be choosers. At least, they had the prospect of a future deliverer. The fact that the deliverer would be 'a son' would have stirred their imagination. For the covenant God of their fathers had always worked from father to son, and that particularly so with David and his heirs, even though now the kingdom was divided and the rival dynasty of Israel established in the north. The fact that the government would be 'on his shoulders' was a bonus. Maybe the kingdom would be reunited and effective control restored to Jerusalem where it ought to be. Later, God through Isaiah promised concerning Eliakim, 'I will place on his shoulder the key to the house of David; what he opens no one can shut, and what he shuts no one can open. I will drive him like a peg into a firm place; he will be a seat of honour for the house of his father' (Isa. 22:22-23). This was what was needed: good, stable government. There was much here to console. The prophecy, even at this early stage, was thoroughly human and completely practical. Whatever the terrors of the present, the people could at least hold on to this word of the Lord for the future.

We can sense the stirrings in Judah as Isaiah brought this message from God. Our understanding of it, however, goes yet further and stirs us even more deeply. We see in the Immanuel prophecy not just a Messianic sign, but the actual promise of Christ's birth (Matt. 1:23). We regard Isaiah's words here as a description of the person and work of Christ. Immediate fulfilment might be seen in Eliakim or later in Hezekiah. The details, however, transcend this and find ultimate completion in Jesus. They point to the God-man and to the kingdom he established.

The divinity of the Messiah

The human side is clear enough: the birth, the child, even the son. But what of the divine? Does the description lead to that conclusion or simply to a human figure who would arise in the succeeding years?

> 'And he will be called
>> Wonderful Counsellor, Mighty God,
>> Everlasting Father, Prince of Peace.
> Of the increase of his government and peace
>> there will be no end.
> He will reign on David's throne
>> and over his kingdom,
> establishing and upholding it
>> with justice and righteousness

from that time on and for ever.
The zeal of the Lord Almighty
    will accomplish this'

(Isa. 9:6-7).

As we consider the names given to the child promised by Isaiah, both against their Old Testament background and in their New Testament fulfilment, they point compellingly to the divine nature of the coming deliverer. On their accession to the throne the Pharaohs of Middle Egypt were hailed with five titles. Names in the Bible meant more than that. They described the character of the one who bore them.

Wonderful Counsellor

The child was called 'Wonderful Counsellor'. In the days of the Judges, Manoah, Samson's father, had that strange encounter with the man of God, who gave him details of Samson's birth and advised about his upbringing. Manoah asked the man his name and was told, 'It is beyond understanding,' or 'Wonderful' (Judg. 13:18). Subsequent events proved to Manoah that the man of God's true identity was 'the angel of the Lord'. Manoah feared death since, in his opinion, he and his wife had seen God. Isaiah himself later described the Lord Almighty as 'wonderful in counsel and magnificent in wisdom' (Isa. 28:29). This 'wonderful counsel' was clearly a divine attribute.

It is precisely this 'wonderful counsel' which Jesus claimed for his teaching. Commenting on the crowd's reluctance to accept the varied approaches of John the Baptist and himself, he maintained that, in spite of their attitude, wisdom was yet justified in her children. He bluntly told his enemies, alluding to himself, that a greater than Solomon was among them. He taught in parables, as the wise men of Old Testament days had taught in proverbs. He described the Spirit who would continue his work as 'another Counsellor' (John 14:16). He claimed that no one knows the Son except the Father, and no one knows the Father except the Son and those to whom the Son chooses to reveal him (Matt. 11:27).

Others recognized the 'wonderful counsel' of Jesus' teaching. His own village folk were amazed at the gracious words he spoke. His hearers were startled at the authority of his teaching. The temple-guards were surprised at the way he taught. The woman of Sychar was shattered by Jesus' detailed knowledge of her life. He must be the Christ. Nicodemus was so gripped by the challenge of the teacher he respected that he queried further the strange information Jesus brought to him. Paul, thinking of the uniqueness of God's salvation in Jesus, quoted from Isaiah: 'Who has known the mind of the Lord? Or who has been his counsellor?' (Rom. 11:34; cf. Isa. 40:13).

We need to recognize the amazing wisdom of Jesus' teaching. In him, Paul reminds us, are hidden all the treasures of wisdom. This came home to me after a series on the Sermon on the Mount in our mid-week Bible Studies. Forced to concentrate on Jesus' teaching, to compare it with the Old Testament and with the teaching of the scribes and Pharisees, we were gripped afresh by the depth of Jesus' wisdom. We discovered its practical implications in a new way. More than that, we began to see how the Old Testament prepared for Christ's teaching and how the New Testament expanded its meaning. We found again the amazing centrality of Jesus' teaching to the whole of Scripture. This is what happens when we study Christ in Isaiah.

Mighty God

His name was also 'Mighty God'. Some have suggested this simply means, 'God-like hero'. But the sense is much stronger. This title includes the Hebrew *El,* one of the names for God, derived from the idea of strength. The title was also used in compounds in the Old Testament as a name for God: *El Shaddai,* the Almighty God; *El Olam,* the Eternal God; *El Roeh,* the All-seeing God. Here it is *El Gibbor,* the Mighty God. Later, Isaiah used the same expression alongside 'the Lord, the Holy One of Israel' (Isa. 10:20,21). This is particularly significant, for 'the Holy One of Israel' is a favourite term of Isaiah's in describing Jehovah. Divinity is implicit in the name, 'the Mighty God'.

Jesus declared his divine nature in the miracles he performed. He used his miraculous 'works' to substantiate his claims. The Jews, however, continued in their unbelief. John comments in his Gospel that this was to fulfil the work of Isaiah the prophet. He quotes Isaiah 53:1 and 6:10 and then adds, 'Isaiah said this because he saw Jesus' glory and spoke about him' (John 12:41). Jesus' claims reached their apex when, confronting the Jewish leaders, he said, 'Before Abraham was born, I am!' (John 8:58). It was one thing to claim superiority over the great religious mentors of their faith, Abraham, Moses and Solomon; it was sheer blasphemy for any man to take on his lips, as a personal claim, the unrepeatable covenant name of God: I AM. That was intolerable. It was for that reason that they picked up stones to deal with this blasphemer. Jesus, the Mighty God, however, hid himself, slipping away from the temple grounds.

The miracles and claims of Jesus are inexplicably bound together. The reaction of the Pharisees to Jesus' healing of a paralytic makes that clear. 'Who is this fellow who speaks blasphemy? Who can forgive sins but God alone?' (Luke 5:21; Mark 2:7). We are not at liberty to pick and choose those miracles or claims most acceptable to our modern minds and discard the rest. Jesus did what he did and claimed to be who he was, and in this he was either mighty God or mistaken man. His words and works testify to his divinity. They belong together. They both witness to his divine person. To reject either of them is to reject the Christ of the Scriptures.

Everlasting Father

The child was named 'Everlasting Father'. This in itself is startling. To the Son is attributed fatherhood, and that endlessly. Behind 'Father' lie ideas of creation, protection and sustenance, as well as fatherly care. The addition of 'everlasting' brings eternity into focus and stresses the divine dimension. God, as Father, is seen in the Old Testament as the author of life and covenant love. These are pre-eminently divine functions. Rabbi Hertz comments: 'This is quite impossible. No true prophet — indeed no true Israelite — would apply a term like "Mighty God" or "Everlasting Father" to any mortal prince.' Sometimes earthly monarchs took the title of father of their people but they seldom lived up to it.

Jesus developed the idea of God's fatherhood in an intriguing way. He stressed the comfort it brings to his followers. They are children of God their heavenly Father. They pray to him to guide them and to provide for their needs. They trust in him to avoid needless anxiety.

Jesus also emphasized his own relationship with God his Father. His Father worked, so he worked. He did only what his Father commanded. All those who came to him did so because his Father brought them. Jesus distinguished between himself and God as persons, and yet stressed an underlying unity. At one critical juncture, when the Jews again picked up stones to stone him as a blasphemer, Jesus claimed, 'I and the Father are one' (John 10:30). This was the measure of the child who was parent, the Son who was Father. Jesus declared what Isaiah amazingly forecast of him in calling him, 'Mighty God, Everlasting Father'.

The comfort of God's fatherhood, which Jesus stressed, is a great blessing. What was hidden, and even secondary, in the Old Testament concerning God's fatherhood, Jesus made open and of primary importance. The rule of God the Father is the rule of a covenant God over a covenant community. Jesus' followers are 'blessed' through God their heavenly Father.

This helps us in our faith as we trust not only a sovereign, but a caring God, who is unchanging and yet so near. It stimulates our prayers to seek God's glory and our own needs, from one who is well able to provide both. It directs our attitude to material things, both present and future, with tranquillity. It moulds our relationships, for Christians are sons and daughters of God our Father and fellow-men are creatures for whom God shows, in common grace, a loving concern.

Jesus' teaching about God's fatherhood also indicates the triune nature of God. The Trinity is not simply a man-made formulation but explains the nature of God and indicates how God brings salvation to man. God sent Jesus and so the Son works. Jesus bequeathed the Spirit and so the work continues. As Paul and Peter were later to teach, the Father initiates, the Son provides and the Spirit applies salvation (Eph.1; 1 Peter 1:1-2). Yet, in all of this, there is underlying unity: 'There are three persons in the Godhead; the Father, the Son and the Holy Ghost; and these three are one God, the same in substance, equal in power and glory' (*Shorter Catechism,* 6).

Prince of Peace

Isaiah's Christ is called 'Prince of Peace'. In the Old Testament, peace meant not only the end of war but total well-being in life. A purely human deliverer might bring about peace, but only God establishes this kind of well-being. Isaiah stresses this by prophesying the eternal nature of government and peace through the Messiah.

Jesus' teaching reflects the tension between human and divine peace to the point of paradox. To his friends on one occasion Jesus said, 'Do not suppose that I have come to bring peace to the earth. I did not come to bring peace, but a sword. For I have come to turn

"a man against his father,
   a daughter against her mother,
a daughter-in-law against her mother-in-law—
   a man's enemies will be the members of his own household"'
                                                   (Matt. 10:34-36; cf. Micah 7:6).

At another time Jesus declared, 'Peace I leave with you; my peace I give you. I do not give to you as the world gives. Do not let your hearts be troubled and do not be afraid' (John 14:27).

Is there a contradiction here? Is Jesus the Prince of Peace or of war? It is precisely because Jesus is the divine Prince of a divine peace that his claims take precedence over all other human relationships. As Messiah, he has not come to defeat the armies of Rome but to rout Satan.

The peace Jesus establishes is divine, not human. E. J. Young comments: 'In active vigour He is the true David and in love of peace the real Solomon.'

John Calvin summarizes forcefully the divinity of these titles: 'Now, to apply this for our instruction, whenever any distrust arises, and all means of escape are taken away from us, whenever in short, it appears to us that everything is in a ruinous condition, let us recall to our remembrance that Christ is called *Wonderful,* because he has inconceivable methods of assisting us and because his power is far beyond what we are able to conceive. When we need counsel, let us remember that he is *the Counsellor.* When we need strength let us remember that he is *Mighty* and *Strong.* When new terrors spring up suddenly every instant and when many deaths threaten us from various quarters, let us rely on that *eternity* of which he is with good reason called the Father and by the same comfort let us learn to soothe all temporal distresses. When we are inwardly tossed by various tempests, and when Satan attempts to disturb our consciences, let us remember that Christ is *the Prince of Peace* and that it is easy for him to quickly allay all our uneasy feelings. Thus will these titles confirm us more and more in the faith of Christ and justify us against Satan and against hell itself.'

The God-man

We have seen, then, from these titles how Isaiah predicts a Christ who is both human and divine. How gloriously these names were fulfilled in the Lord Jesus! We use the description 'God-man' for this. It is a good phrase, for it combines both ideas in one word, just as both natures, human and divine, are combined in one person, the Lord Jesus Christ. As a child Christ was born; as a son he was given. For Paul, he was the Son, 'who as to his human nature was a descendant of David, and who through the Spirit of holiness was declared with power to be the Son of God, by his resurrection from the dead' (Rom. 1:3; cf. Gal. 4:4).

It is as God-man that Isaiah's Christ penetrates the darkness with light, shatters the bondage of slavery and establishes his kingly rule amid chaos. This last aspect, as we have seen, is the one Isaiah stresses towards the close of his message. The rule, however, is established not only through the divine Messiah, but is brought about through the Messiah's kingdom. Not only the person of Christ, but the work of Christ is involved. Isaiah details that work as the present oracle ends:

'Of the increase of his government and peace
   there will be no end.
He will reign on David's throne
   and over his kingdom,
establishing and upholding it
   with justice and righteousness
   from that time on and for ever.
The zeal of the Lord Almighty
   will accomplish this'

(Isa. 9:7).

There is a kind of crescendo in Isaiah's words which was bound to stir the hearts of Judah. It moved like a great symphony to a climax — not only a child, but a son; not only a son, but a king; not only a king, but a king on David's throne; not only for now, but for ever. Each time I listen to the chorus from Handel's *Messiah,* 'For unto us a child is born', I sense that crescendo as it moves from the rushed beginning to its grand close. It reminds me that the kingdom of God is growing and living, not static, and that eventually God will put everything under Christ's feet.

The throne of David

The mention of 'David's throne' would have been particularly encouraging. There had been little stability in Judah since King Uzziah died. But many who heard Isaiah would have remembered those times, days of settled government, abundant prosperity and relative peacefulness. Now Isaiah was promising even better times with the mention of 'David's throne'. A longing for the recent past was only one motivation. A far more important thing was God's great promise to David. Judah always guarded that promise jealously. In days of civil strife and of a divided kingdom, they had always that promise to cling to. The mention of 'David's throne' brought that, above all, to mind.

'The Lord declares to you that the Lord himself will establish a house for you: When your days are over and you rest with your fathers, I will raise up your offspring to succeed you, who will come from your own body, and I will establish his kingdom. He is the one who will build a house for my Name, and I will establish the throne of his kingdom for ever. I will be his father, and he shall be my son. When he does wrong, I will punish him with the rod of men, with floggings inflicted by men. But my love will never be taken away from him, as I took it away from Saul, whom I removed from before you. Your house and your kingdom shall endure for ever before me; your throne shall be established for ever' (2 Sam. 7:11-16).

Many of the things mentioned here were echoed in Isaiah's words — a stable dynasty, a continuing throne, a father-son relationship. This last made it such an impressive promise. God would be a Father to David and to his son, even 'for ever'. God, in a solemn promise, a covenant, had entered into a relationship with Abraham to be his God and the God of his children. God had renewed and confirmed that relationship with Moses and with the nation of Israel. Here, God promised to be a Father to David, Israel's king, and to his son. This all seemed to fit together, a kind of unfolding plan of God's promise for his people. David himself eventually viewed God's promise to him as a 'covenant' (2 Sam. 23:5; Ps. 89:3-4). Isaiah was now contributing to that unfolding plan, predicting that a child would be born who would rule on David's throne 'for ever', defining that government as being characterized by 'justice and righteousness'. Isaiah was recalling the extent and forecasting the quality of the Messiah's kingdom. John Calvin comments: 'Now this continuance, of which Isaiah now speaks, consists of two parts. It belongs both to time and to quality.'

The fulfilment

The way in which Isaiah's prophecy was fulfilled in the coming of Christ is both strange and impressive. The clearest point of reference is found in Gabriel's words to Mary: 'Do not be afraid, Mary, you have found favour with God. You will be with child and give birth to a son, and you are to give him the name Jesus. He will be great and will be called the Son of the Most High. The Lord God will give him the throne of his father David and he will reign over the house of Jacob for ever; his kingdom will never end' (Luke 1:30-33).

Other parts of the New Testament make clear that the awaited Messiah is the 'Son of David' and identify that Messiah as Jesus of Nazareth. The birth stories in the Gospels affirm this. Blind men call on Jesus' help in this way. The crowd acclaim Jesus' entry to Jerusalem with similar words. The people, discussing on another occasion whether or not Jesus is the Christ, look for a Messiah from David's family and from David's town. Peter, on the Day of Pentecost in Jerusalem, and Paul later, at Antioch, proclaim Christ's resurrection as a fulfilment of David's words in Psalm 16. Twice in his letters Paul describes Jesus as David's descendant. John sees on Patmos a vision of Jesus as the Lion of the tribe of Judah, the key, the root and the offspring of David. It is an impressive array of evidence.

The silence of Christ

The strange thing about all this is the attitude of Jesus himself. During his earthly ministry he is the silent exception. True, he does not oppose others who address him as Son of David. He even accepts and commends Peter's confession that he is the Christ, but then immediately forbids his disciples to publish the fact. He directs others, whom he heals, to the same silence. In public life he throws a cloak of secrecy over the matter of his being the Christ. Only once does he hint at this designation as he poses his Jewish enemies the question: how could Christ be the son of David if David addresses him as Lord? Jesus' own preferred title is Son of Man, not Son of David. Only at the very end of his ministry, when put under oath before Caiaphas, does Jesus admit publicly that he is the Christ.

Why did Jesus behave in this way? Why did he not take the opportunity of identifying with, and even proclaiming, this great and popular perception of Christ as the Son of David? Why did he not openly declare during his earthly ministry, when it would have been most advantageous, that he was David's Son who had come to sit on David's throne and rule over the house of Jacob for ever, instead of leaving it until later, as when he revealed it to John on the island of Patmos?

The reason for Jesus' attitude is both important and instructive. Jesus acted in this way because the current expectation of a Christ who was 'Son of David' was unacceptable to him. He had not come to throw off the yoke of Roman oppression. When the people would have taken Jesus and made him king, he would have none of it. Jesus taught about the kingdom of God mainly in parables and the gist of much of this teaching was the hiddenness and secrecy of the kingdom: the seed growing secretly, the hidden treasure, the wheat and the weeds. Jesus told Peter to sheath his sword, for those who live by the sword would die by the sword. Pilate must learn about a kingdom of truth, said Jesus, for Christ's kingdom was not of this world. Otherwise, Jesus' servants would be fighting for him.

Jesus' studied silence on 'David's son' and 'David's throne' was because he rejected the political and materialistic views of the Messiah and of Messiah's kingdom that were so prevalent in his day. The rule he had come to establish was to be built upon justice and righteousness in the hearts of men. The deliverance he brought was from the chaos of sin, not from civil disorder or from the disruption of foreign oppression. This does not mean that his kingdom has no ethical or moral implications for men and for nations. It undoubtedly has. But it is a spiritual, not a political or a material kingdom. It is a kingdom not of meat and drink but of righteousness, peace and joy in the Holy Ghost. All theologies, liberation theology included, must recognize this. Jesus was reinterpreting messiahship, delivering it from debased views. His kingdom was spiritual.

Jesus' kingdom was also covenantal. His kingdom fulfilled the great promises of God to his people. The thread of that has already been emerging. God's covenant with Abraham, Moses and David has now a forward Messianic thrust in Isaiah and it is this promise of a Messiah that Jesus fulfils in himself. Jesus was born in line with God's covenant with Abraham, died offering his blood as that of the new covenant and was raised from death through the everlasting covenant. The blessing of Abraham has come to the Gentiles through Jesus the Messiah. In this great unfolding saga of salvation, Isaiah had a formative part. Isaiah's Christ fulfilled it. Covenant and kingdom are inseparably joined.

The certainty of Christ's coming

Isaiah's Christ comes. He penetrates the darkness with light, redeems from the slavery of sin and establishes through his kingdom the rule of order in place of chaos. Isaiah's words may have had a partial fulfilment in his own day but they only found their ultimate completion in the coming of Christ. The mysterious unfinished data of the Old and the precise completed detail of the New Testament Scriptures make this plain.

> The race that long in darkness pin'd
> Have seen a glorious light;
> The people dwell in day, who dwelt
> In death's surrounding night.
>
> To hail thy rise, thou better Sun!
> The gath'ring nations come,
> Joyous, as when the reapers bear
> The harvest treasures home.
>
> For thou our burden hast remov'd
> And quell'd th'oppressor's sway,
> Quick as the slaughter'd squadrons fell
> In Midian's evil day.
>
> To us a Child of hope is born;
> To us a Son is giv'n;
> Him shall the tribes of earth obey,
> Him all the hosts of heav'n.

His name shall be the Prince of Peace,
For evermore ador'd,
The Wonderful, the Counsellor,
The great and mighty Lord.

His pow'r increasing still shall spread,
His reign no end shall know;
Justice shall guard his throne above,
And peace abound below.

(Scottish Paraphrases)

'The zeal of the Lord Almighty will accomplish this' (Isa. 9:7). This marked the grand finale of Isaiah's oracle on the coming of Christ. God's zeal is his burning commitment to accomplish his will. The disciples noted this same zeal in Jesus in relation to God's house (John 2:17). The coming of Isaiah's Christ was certain. The Lord Almighty was committed to it. The Christ would definitely come. Of that there could be no doubt.

2.
The kingdom of Christ

Isaiah had predicted the coming of Christ very clearly. As we have seen, the birth of the Immanuel child points forwards to Christ the Word coming to dwell among his people. When Christ comes, he will penetrate the darkness of sin with light, liberate those enslaved by sin's power and bring order out of the chaos caused by sin. This was all fulfilled in the life and ministry of Jesus. Indeed, the way in which Jesus used Isaiah's thoughts and words emphasizes the importance of the prophet's predictions in his mind.

A successful King

The prophecy continues. Isaiah 11:1-5 proclaims the character of the coming Christ in such a way that the glory of his kingdom is evident. Christ will be a King whose reign is prosperous: 'A shoot will come up from the stump of Jesse; from his roots a Branch will bear fruit' (Isa. 11:1).

The stump of Jesse

The King, however, will have lowly beginnings. The description 'stump of Jesse' is a strange one. It is as though all the greatness of David's kingdom is eclipsed and his once glorious name as founder of the dynasty is not worth mentioning. The lineage has returned to the obscurity of the household of Jesse at the time when Samuel sought out the red-faced youth to anoint him king. Gone were the hopes of God's promise to David and his son, so plainly evident in the glory of Solomon's temple. The dynasty of David was now the remaining stump of Jesse. The 'roots' were 'a dry stock'. There was little in the description that was uplifting.

This, of course, was the vein in which Isaiah had just been speaking. Destruction would be widespread. The metaphor of the forest is used:

'See, the Lord, the Lord Almighty,
    will lop off the boughs with great power.
The lofty trees will be felled,
    the tall ones will be brought low.
He will cut down the forest thickets with an axe;
    Lebanon will fall before the Mighty One'

(Isa. 10:33-34).

Isaiah is using the imagery of 11:1 in terms of contrast rather than similarity. The stump of Jesse, which was now like those felled stocks of Lebanon, would yet one day bear fruit.

Isaiah would have recalled the terms of God's commission to him:

'But as the terebinth and oak
    leave stumps when they are cut down,
    so the holy seed will be the stump in the land'

(Isa. 6:13).

But here the 'stump of Jesse' speaks of the small beginnings of Messiah's kingdom. We need to pause and reflect on the humble origins of the Messianic King. Calvin stresses the fulfilment of this prophecy in Jesus Christ alone: 'Hence we infer that this prediction applies solely to the person of Christ; for till he came no such *branch* arose. It certainly cannot be applied to Hezekiah or Josiah, who, from their very infancy, were brought up in the expectation of occupying a throne. Zerubbabel (Ezra 3:8) did not attain the thousandth part of that elevated rank which the Prophet extols.'

Positively, the small beginnings of Messiah's kingdom can be applied to Jesus. The details of his birth make this clear. Though descended from David and pressed by that necessity to enrol in the census at Bethlehem, Joseph and his betrothed Mary are so unimportant as to be lodged in the outhouse, not the inn. Apart from the visit of the wise men and local shepherds, the birth of Jesus attracts little attention. Some years later, as the family travel home from the temple, they appear simply as one family among other pilgrims on the caravan route home. Joseph may have been an upright man, but he was a very ordinary man too.

The area of Jesus' upbringing is not only obscure but despised from a Messianic point of view. No prophet was ever expected to come from Galilee. Indeed, that fact put a big question mark in many minds over the very idea of Jesus being Messiah. Nathaniel is scathing about Nazareth: 'Can anything good come from there?' (John 1:46). The Jewish leaders are of the same mind (John 7:52).

The ordinariness of Jesus' family is noted. Amazement soon gives way to incredulity and criticism as Jesus speaks in his home synagogue at Nazareth. 'Joseph's son', 'Mary's boy', 'the carpenter', 'the carpenter's son', 'the brother of James, Joses, Judas and Simon', 'his sisters living among us' are the comments of the village folk as they question Jesus' wisdom and his right to address them. This prophet certainly had no honour in his own country.

The interesting feature, from our point of view, is that Luke notes the occasion of this criticism as directly following Jesus' teaching in the Nazareth synagogue when he read from the prophet Isaiah and had the audacity, in the view of some, to apply the fulfilment of that scripture to himself:

> '"The Spirit of the Lord is on me,
> 	because he has anointed me
> 	to preach good news to the poor.
> He has sent me to proclaim freedom for the prisoners
> 	and recovery of sight for the blind,
> to release the oppressed
> 	to proclaim the year of the Lord's favour" ...

The eyes of everyone in the synagogue were fastened on him, and he began by saying to them, "Today this scripture is fulfilled in your hearing"' (Luke 4:18 -21; cf. v. 28; Isa. 61:1-2).

There is an important lesson here for us in Christian work. So often today in Christian circles big is beautiful. Mammoth plans, massive meetings, national campaigns, countless decisions for Christ are the order of the day. We must, of course, have enlarged vision. We need to see with the eyes of faith. We must recognize the vast number of people who have no church connection and little thought of God, and we need to take steps to win them for Christ. But we must surely not be duped into thinking that the answer lies simply in organizing mission campaigns on as large a scale as possible. The biblical teaching about the origin and growth of Christ's kingdom points in a different direction.

We find here a shoot rising from the stump of Jesse. God wants us to recognize the hopelessness of the gospel situation from a human point of view and to turn to him for help. From obscure beginnings,

Jesus' ministry got under way. He spent time in prayer, taught, healed and helped people. He trained a small group of followers. He claimed that his kingdom, from the smallest of beginnings, would eventually become great. Times of revival, such as on the Day of Pentecost, among the Samaritan community or in Cornelius' home, still lay in the future. These were to be special times of intensive and immediate growth. But the inauguration of the kingdom was a relatively quiet affair.

God does not despise the day of small things, and neither should we. Reviewing my own ministry, I am saddened by the lack of fruitfulness and constantly question myself about prayer, zeal and proper priorities. Having sincerely done that, however, I remind myself that, except for special times of blessing, the growth pattern will be of the order of the seed in the soils — hard, stony, thorny and good (Mark 4:1-20). When the church follows the pattern of Christ's ministry and teaching, it knows purposeful activity, steady growth and divine blessing. Otherwise, it faces frustration and disappointment on the one side, or superficial success on the other.

The Branch

While the Messianic King would have lowly beginnings, his kingly rule would ultimately be successful. From the imagery of the forest, with its felled stumps, the picture of a fruitful branch now comes into view: 'From his roots a Branch will bear fruit' (Isa. 11:1).

Isaiah has already predicted a day when 'The Branch of the Lord will be beautiful and glorious, and the fruit of the land will be the pride and glory of the survivors in Israel' (Isa. 4:2). The idea of 'the Branch', a shoot cut for grafting, from the house of David, eventually became an accepted term for the coming Messiah. Other prophets mention this. Jeremiah's 'Branch' anticipated the righteousness of the Messianic King, Zechariah's, the cleansing of the Messianic Priest (Jer. 23:5; 33:15; Zech. 3:8; 6:12). Jewish writings like the *Targum* and rabbinical literature, as well as members of the Qumran community, a sect in early Christian times, used the term 'branch' or 'shoot' for the Messiah.

Isaiah speaks of the prosperity and success of the Messianic branch. The same is true here in 11:1 as in 4:2. From widespread devastation and destruction, a shoot will sprout from the stump of Jesse and become a fruitful branch. This tender shoot, rising like a root out of dry ground, will eventually become an oak of righteousness, a planting of the Lord. The felled stump of Lebanon will witness a growth in arid circumstances which will redound to God's glory (Isa. 53:2 ; 61:3).

Isaiah uses different words for 'branch' in these two sayings. In 4:2

it is the Hebrew *semah*; in 11:1, the term *neser*. While differing little in meaning, the latter word may well be significant in the light of Matthew's Gospel. One of Matthew's comments has always posed a problem: 'And he went and lived in a town called Nazareth. So was fulfilled what was said through the prophets: "He will be called a Nazarene"' (Matt. 2:23). The difficulty is in finding this precise prediction in the prophets, for certainly, in that form, it does not appear. Matthew would hardly be suggesting that Jesus was a 'Nazarite', having taken the strict vows of this Jewish order, for Jesus did not do this. It is much more likely to be a play on the word *neser*. *Neser* has a similar sound to 'Nazareth'. Nazareth, Jesus' home village, the place where his Messianic claims were strongly questioned, and Galilee, the wider area, from which no messiah was ever expected to come, became the place in which God caused the shoot to burst from the stump. Was Matthew thinking of this when he said, 'He will be called a Nazarene'?

Fruitfulness characterized Christ's kingdom. We see this as we recall Jesus' ministry. At two points in his teaching it is particularly clear — the parable of the mustard seed and the allegory of the vine. Isaiah spoke of a fruitful branch. Ezekiel speaks of Israel in terms of God planting a shoot which grows into a mighty cedar where the birds nest (Ezek. 17:22-24). Jesus may have had both prophecies in mind as he told the parable of the mustard seed and taught the allegory of the vine: 'The kingdom of heaven is like a mustard seed, which a man took and planted in his field. Though it is the smallest of all your seeds, yet when it grows, it is the largest of the garden plants and becomes a tree, so that the birds of the air come and perch in its branches' (Matt. 13:31-32).

The *small beginnings* of the kingdom are evident here. Its extensive growth is marked. The protection and benefit for the birds, the most dependent of creatures, is a significant purpose of that growth. All these features relate to Isaiah's prediction of the growth of Christ's kingdom.

The allegory of the vine drives the truth yet deeper (John 15:1-8). In the Old Testament, Israel is described as a vine. The people are God's planting. So, implicit in the fruitfulness of the Messianic Branch are the benefits which come to Christians through Christ. Jesus emphasizes this in his teaching about the vine. He is the genuine vine. God is the gardener who trims and prunes the vine. Christians are branches linked to the vine and bearing fruit as a result.

Jesus said that the branches must remain in the vine. In this way they bear fruit and so prove to be his disciples. This is the proof of true discipleship, the test to be applied to false teachers. By their fruits we shall know them. People do not gather grapes from thorns or figs from thistles (Matt. 7:16). Fruit is the natural and necessary outcome of growth.

Jesus also instructs his followers how they can bear fruit: 'If you remain in me and my words remain in you, ask whatever you wish, and it will be given you. This is to my Father's glory, that you bear much fruit, showing yourselves to be my disciples' (John 15:7-8). How helpful this is! The bald command to remain in Christ might inspire our obedience, but it does not indicate the method. Without the method, it leads only to frustration. Christ, however, points out the way. He directs to the Word and prayer. As we remain in his Word, he speaks to us and directs our praying to him in response. This process produces growth and fruitfulness in our lives. It is a continuing process of obedience, of abiding in him.

All of these features — the nature, necessity and blessing of the fruitfulness of the kingdom of Christ — are predicted in Isaiah's Branch. This kind of growth is the natural outcome of a relationship with Jesus the Messiah. As Christians, fruitfulness in character is the proof of our profession and our primary means of witness. By this, the world judges whether or not our claim to be Christian is genuine. By this, we test the credibility of our own profession of faith and make our calling and election sure. It is neither our ability to speak about our faith, nor our standing in church life, but the fruit of the Spirit in our lives which shows above all the reality of our Christian profession. The church must never forget this.

Most gratifying of all, however, is the fact that this fruitfulness comes to us as a gift from Christ. His fruitfulness is transferred to our lives. The benefits of Christ the King come to the members of Christ's kingdom. Christ's rule in us produces fruit in our lives. This is not only the implication of the opening words of this prophecy, but its continuing theme. The lowly origin and prosperous outcome of Isaiah's King and his kingdom are for the benefit of the King's subjects.

> Saviour, sprinkle many nations,
> Fruitful let thy sorrows be;
> By thy pains and consolations
> Draw the Gentiles unto thee.
>
> Of thy cross the wondrous story,
> Be it to the nations told;
> Let them see thee in thy glory
> And thy mercy manifold.
>
>   (Arthur Cleveland Coxe)

An equipped Messiah

Isaiah's Christ will be a Messiah perfectly equipped to rule:

'The Spirit of the Lord will rest on him—
  the Spirit of wisdom and of understanding,
  the Spirit of counsel and of power,
  the Spirit of knowledge and of the fear of the Lord—
and he will delight in the fear of the Lord'

(Isa. 11:2-3).

The anointing of the Spirit

Isaiah predicts that 'the Spirit of the Lord will rest' on the coming King. This would equip him for office and empower him for government. The visual token of this authority in the Old Testament was anointing with oil. Both things and people were anointed, and this meant that they were 'set apart' or 'holy' to God, separated for God's use alone. It was a criminal offence to compound holy oil for a common purpose. Prophets, priests and kings were all anointed as a sign of their being set apart to God's service. The Hebrew word for 'anointed' is *Mashiah*, the Greek *Christos*. From these, come our English terms 'Messiah' and 'Christ', which have the same basic meaning.

Isaiah does not use the term 'anointed' here, but he does use it later:

'The Spirit of the Sovereign Lord is on me,
  because the Lord has anointed me
  to preach good news to the poor'

(Isa. 61:1).

However, the idea of anointing by the Spirit is quite plain in 11:2, even if the actual word is not used. What Isaiah stresses at this point is that the Spirit of the Lord will rest on the coming King. By this, he means that God's Spirit will remain in an abiding way on him. This is important. Frequently, in Old Testament times, God's Spirit came spasmodically, or periodically, on people to equip them for service. We see this especially in the case of Samson, as we read of enormous strength coming to him at critical junctures just when he needed it. On Isaiah's King, God's Spirit will remain. The Messiah, God's anointed one, will be characterized by the continuing presence of God's Spirit, not in any temporary or partial way. Have we here a reference in the Old Testament to the triune nature of God? The Lord, the Spirit and the Messiah are all mentioned in this context.

Luke stresses the fulfilment of this great prediction. He locates the anointing of the human Jesus with the Spirit of God at his baptism. The details are intriguing. Matthew, Mark and Luke all describe the Spirit coming down on Jesus like a dove at his baptism and record the words of divine sanction: 'You are my Son, whom I love; with you I am well pleased' (Matt. 3:16-17; Mark 1:9-11; Luke 3:21-22). Luke goes on to note how Jesus was about thirty years old when he began his ministry (Luke 3:23). This was the age at which priests in the Old Testament were anointed for service. He lists Jesus' ancestry as though to affirm his genealogical claim to office (Luke 3:24-38). He recalls how Jesus, 'full of the Holy Spirit, returned from the Jordan and was led by the Spirit' to the desert temptations (Luke 4:1). He then recounts how he 'returned to Galilee in the power of the Spirit' (Luke 4:14), went into his home synagogue in Nazareth, and read from Isaiah the words:

> 'The Spirit of the Lord is on me,
>   because he has anointed me
>   to preach good news to the poor . . .'

applying this prophecy boldly to himself: 'Today this scripture is fulfilled in your hearing.' Luke then immediately records how Jesus exorcised an evil spirit, as though to give positive proof of the power of God's Spirit upon him (Luke 4:31-36).

Is Luke suggesting here that the anointing of Jesus by God's Spirit at his baptism was an abiding feature continuing through the Spirit's direction of Christ throughout his ministry? In Acts, Luke picks up that telling description of Christ, as Peter preaches in Cornelius' home about 'how God anointed Jesus of Nazareth with the Holy Spirit and power, and how he went around doing good and healing all who were under the power of the devil, because God was with him' (Acts 10:38). Luke confirms in his history what he stresses in his Gospel of the abiding power of God's Spirit on the anointed Jesus in his work.

It is the human Jesus who was anointed by the Spirit, not the divine Son. We need to keep this in mind. It is inconceivable that the divine Son would need such anointing, even though we are left with the problem of an anointing occurring in the one person of Christ with divine and human natures. Paul reminds us of that plenitude of divine power in the human Jesus: 'For in Christ all the fulness of the Deity lives in bodily form' (Col. 2:9).

Again, it is Calvin who emphasizes this point particularly to show the relevance of Christ's anointing with the Spirit for his people: 'We must keep in view what I mentioned a little ago, that this refers to Christ's human nature; because he could not be enriched with the gift and grace of the Father, except so far as he became man. Besides, as he came down to us, so he received the gifts of *the Spirit,* that he might bestow them on us. And this is the *anointing* from which he receives the name of *Christ,* which he imparts to us; for why are we called *Christians,* but because he admits us into his fellowship, by distributing to us out of his fulness *according to the measure* (Eph. 4:7) of undeserved liberality? And undoubtedly this passage does not so much teach us what Christ is in himself, as what he received from the Father, that he might enrich us with his wealth.'

The anointing of believers

It is because Christ was anointed by the Spirit that Christians are anointed by the Spirit. There are two places in the New Testament where believers are described as anointed by the Spirit: 'Now it is God who makes both us and you stand firm in Christ. He anointed us, set his seal of ownership on us, and put his Spirit in our hearts as a deposit, guaranteeing what is to come' (2 Cor. 1:21-22). 'But you have an anointing from the Holy One, and all of you know the truth... As for you, the anointing you received from him remains in you, and you do not need anyone to teach you. But as his anointing teaches you about all things and as that anointing is real, not counterfeit — just as it has taught you, remain in him' (1 John 2:20, 27).

This anointing is universal. It is for all believers. It is not for a minority, or a spiritual élite, but is the mark and possession of all Christians. Paul includes himself and the Corinthian church, with all its faults, in this. John writes specifically to those who know the truth, a description he uses for Christians.

The anointing is original in the sense that it relates to their experience of becoming Christians, and is not something subsequent to it. Paul writes of their present experience, their standing firm in Christ, as the result of past blessings, their having been anointed, sealed and guaranteed. John speaks of what they have heard 'from the beginning' remaining in his readers. Their anointing is related to this knowledge (1 John 2:24). This anointing is something Christians receive at conversion, not some time after it.

The anointing is an abiding feature, like that of the Spirit resting on the Messiah (Isa. 11:2). It is identified with a seal of ownership and a deposit guaranteeing what is to come, both being of permanent validity. The anointing they received remains in them. The anointing is also related to knowledge. It is real, not counterfeit, for it is based on truth. Paul reminds the Corinthians of their knowledge of the promises of God fulfilled in Christ (2 Cor.1:20). John tells his readers, in language reminiscent of the Paraclete's ministry (John 16:13), that this anointing teaches them about all things (1 John 2:27).

The anointing of the Spirit belongs to all who become Christians. It informs their minds in the knowledge of the truth. It assures their hearts of their fellowship with Christ. It is confirmed by the fruit of the Spirit in their lives. Of this E. H. Andrews writes, 'John's message seems to be that true assurance stems from the Spirit's witness in the heart but that this inner witness must be confirmed by the fruits of righteousness in the believer's life. The balance is excellent. The external tests protect us from the danger of self-delusion, while the inner witness protects us from legalism and assures the believing heart of the Father-child relationship which exists between God and the Christian. "See how great a love the Father has bestowed upon us," cries John, "that we should be called children of God, and such we are" (1 John 3:1).'

As the Spirit's anointing of the Messiah led to a host of attributes equipping him for office, so Christ's anointing leads not only to the anointing of his people, but, as proof of this, to the fruit of the Spirit in their lives. In fellowship with Christ we are anointed by the Spirit, abidingly and effectively.

> Hail to the Lord's Anointed,
> Great David's greater Son!
> Hail, in the time appointed,
> His reign on earth begun!
> He comes to break oppression,
> To set the captive free,
> To take away transgression,
> And rule in equity.
>
> For him shall prayer unceasing
> And daily vows ascend,
> His kingdom still increasing,
> A kingdom without end.
> The mountain dews shall nourish
> A seed, in weakness sown,
> Whose fruit shall spread and flourish
> And shake like Lebanon.
>
> O'er every foe victorious,
> He on his throne shall rest,
> From age to age more glorious,
> All blessing and all blest.

The tide of time shall never
His covenant remove;
His name shall stand for ever;
That name to us is love.

                                                    (James Montgomery)

The attributes which accompany the anointing

It is not only the anointing of the Spirit of the Lord which shows the
glory and splendour of Isaiah's Messiah, but also the attributes which
accompany this anointing.

'The Spirit of the Lord will rest on him—
   the Spirit of wisdom and of understanding,
   the Spirit of counsel and of power
   the Spirit of knowledge and of the fear of the Lord—
and he will delight in the fear of the Lord'

                                                    (Isa.11:2-3).

The way in which these attendant characteristics is expressed is
worth noting. It is as though the central feature was 'the Spirit of the
Lord' himself. Branching from this are three groups of couplets
marking the Messiah's anointed life and work — wisdom and
understanding, counsel and power, knowledge and the fear of the Lord.
H. C. Leupold suggests that the image of the lampstand may in part have
inspired the oracle: 'The seven-branched lampstand of the tabernacle
of days of old may be the type that furnished the illustration involved.'
   That certainly seems to have been the case with the prophet
Zechariah at a later time. In a vision, through which the prophet reminds
Zerubbabel that it is not by might nor by power but by God's Spirit that
the building of the temple will be completed, Zechariah sees a solid
gold lampstand with seven lights on it placed between two olive trees.
In the subsequent explanation of the vision, the lampstand represents
God's Spirit and the two olive trees 'the two who are anointed to serve
the Lord of all the earth' — Zerubbabel the king and Joshua the priest.
The relevance of Zechariah's vision is all the more telling for Isaiah's
word when we recall that Zechariah had just previously predicted the
coming of the Messiah under the imagery of 'the Branch' (Zech. 3:8 ;
4:1-14; 6:12).
   More important than the form of Isaiah's prediction is the
significance of these attributes of the Spirit of God in the life of the
anointed Messiah. The grouping in twos of these characteristics helps
us understand their meaning. The first of each couplet describes an

inherent quality or mark of the Spirit's anointing. The second traces out the practical expression of the attribute, the ability to implement the gift.

'Wisdom' is a comprehensive insight into every aspect of life. 'Understanding' is the faculty of forming a proper judgement on the basis of such wisdom. 'Counsel' is the determining of a plan of action. 'Power' is the means by which the plan is carried into effect. 'Knowledge' is a universal awareness of God, not simply at an intellectual, but at a personal level. 'Fear' is the resultant attitude of reverence towards God arising from this knowledge. The format reaches a climax in the closing expression: 'And he will delight in the fear of the Lord.' The translation 'delight' means literally 'to give a keen smell'. It is as though the anointed Messiah will have an instinctive sensitivity for revering God and will take pleasure in only those things which please God. The phrase is similar to, but stronger than, the one used in Psalm 1:2: 'But his delight is in the law of the Lord.' The same idea occurs in Psalm 40:8: 'I desire to do your will, O my God; your law is within my heart.'

This perfectly amplifies the meaning. The knowledge of God will be so much a part of the anointed Messiah's nature that he will seek to please God and will take great delight in doing so. We see here both a trait of character rooted deep in the Messiah's nature and a consequent practical expression of the same in daily life — a knowledge which produces fear, just as the wisdom leads to understanding and the counsel to power. It is a gift which is real, a fruit which finds natural and effective expression.

This was fulfilled in Jesus of Nazareth, anointed with the Holy Spirit and power, who 'went around doing good and healing all who were under the power of the devil, because God was with him' (Acts 10:38). Here is the essential dwelling of God the Spirit in Jesus' goodness and the expression of this in his ability to heal the sick and exorcise demons. It was also exemplified in Jesus' life of obedience to God his Father. He did only the things the Father commanded. His Father worked, so he worked. His words were not his own, but his Father's who sent him. His prayers were directed to his Father's glory, a glory which they enjoyed before his incarnation. His will was submitted to his Father in the pain of Gethsemane and Calvary. The whole purpose of his life was to please God and to bring about God's glory. To this end wisdom and understanding, counsel and might, knowledge and fear combined in Jesus' life. They were evident in his youth, clear in his ministry, supreme in his death and strong to the end. They were not simply marks of his character, a visionary's unfulfilled dream. He finished the work his Father gave him to do because, anointed by the Spirit, he had the power and ability to do so.

The gifts and fruit of the Spirit

This pattern is not only evident in the ministry of the anointed Jesus; it is also fulfilled in the life of the church — that is, it affects the nature of Christ's kingdom. Already we have seen how the anointing of Jesus leads to the anointing of his followers by the Spirit. Here we note how the features of Christ's anointing are reproduced in the experience of Christians.

The focus of this fulfilment is in both the gifts and fruit of the Spirit. One of the earliest indications of the Spirit's gifts occurs in the Jerusalem church, as the Seven were appointed to deal with the widows' fund (Acts 6:1-7). The notable feature here, from our point of view, is that the men to be chosen, and actually selected, were described as being full of the Holy Spirit, wisdom, faith, power and grace. These features detail not only authentic marks of Christian character, but the effective expression of these in their work. It is remarkable that men called to a specifically administrative and financial task in the church were required to have, and actually possessed, such high 'spiritual' qualities.

The same duality is evident in other lists of the Spirit's gifts. Paul commends the variety of gifts as he writes to the church at Rome — prophecy, serving, teaching, encouraging, contributing and leadership — but stresses the efficiency and zeal with which these must be carried out: in proportion to one's faith, with generosity, diligence and cheerfulness (Rom. 12:6-8). In the Corinthian church, the inherent qualities of wisdom, knowledge and faith must be combined with expertise in exercising the gifts — healing, miraculous powers, ability to distinguish and interpret tongues (1 Cor. 12:7-11). The gifts of office — apostles, prophets, evangelists, pastor/teachers — are for the practical purpose of preparing God's people for works of service and maturing believers in the faith and knowledge of Christ (Eph. 4:7-13).

The fruit of the Spirit follows a similar pattern, evident both in moral character and holiness of life, displayed in the presence of the ninefold fruit of the Spirit, an apt description of the character and life of Jesus (Gal. 5:22-23). The growth required embraces not only faith, knowledge, godliness and love, but also furnishes the virtues of goodness, self-control, perseverance and brotherly kindness (2 Peter 1:5-9).

All of this shows that the blessing of Christ's anointing affects the nature and behaviour of Christ's kingdom. The benefits we receive as Christians from our Redeemer include an anointing of the Spirit, producing gifts and graces in our lives. Moral transformation will take place in our character and become evident in godly behaviour in daily living. 'For the kingdom of God is not a matter of eating and drinking, but of righteousness, peace and joy in the Holy Spirit' (Rom. 14:17).

A just Judge

Isaiah proclaims a Messianic Judge whose declarations are just:

> 'He will not judge by what he sees with his eyes,
>   or decide by what he hears with his ears;
> but with righteousness he will judge the needy,
>   with justice he will give decisions for the poor of the earth.
> He will strike the earth with the rod of his mouth;
>   with the breath of his lips he will slay the wicked.
> Righteousness will be his belt
>   and faithfulness the sash round his waist'
>
> (Isa. 11:3-5).

The function of a judge

Kings of Israel had to do two things in particular: to lead their people in battle and to administer justice and government. Commenting on this passage J. Skinner notes, 'The Hebrew conception of kingship includes two functions, leadership in war and the administration of justice in time of peace (1 Samuel 8:20). Here, for an obvious reason (ch. 9:5), only the civil aspect of the office is dwelt upon.' The judiciary was an integral part of the function of Israel's king.

The administration of the law and the giving of just judgements was evident from the earliest days in Israel's leadership. Moses was told that he would wear himself out if he carried this workload alone. So elders were appointed to assist him. They heard less complex disputes and referred the more difficult cases to Moses. The 'judges' at a later time carried out legal duties among others. Eventually, from the elders at the city gate to the king on his throne, a system of law developed among God's people. David's expertise in this field is noted. Solomon's wisdom is also evident here. The psalmist prays that God will give the king 'judgements', that is, the ability to judge, to give decisions marked by equity and justice.

In a real sense, this laid the basis of what later came to be known as 'constitutional monarchy'. Constitutional monarchy helped avoid the tyranny of despotism, for the king was not 'above the law'. It was further exemplified in Israel's experience by the fact that the king not only administered law in terms of judicial process, but did this on the basis of God's law. Part of his responsibility as king was to see that God's law was obeyed, as well as to obey it himself.

It was natural, then, that the Messianic King would be portrayed as a judge. N. H. Snaith writes, 'In the [Old Testament] God delegates his function of judge on earth in part to the Messianic prince who is destined to establish the earthly kingdom. When therefore the idea of the Day of the Lord develops, we get parallel with it the idea that the Son of Man will be the judge of all men, so that in the [New Testament] and in the Creeds of the Church it is normally declared that Christ will "come again with glory to judge both the quick and the dead".'

It is natural in terms of Israel's kingship to anticipate the Messiah as Judge. The significant thing in our study is to note the way the function of judgement is delegated to the Messiah alone and how the Son of Man as Judge is related to the Messianic Judge of Isaiah's prediction.

Christ as Judge

Jesus himself makes it clear that judgement has been delegated to him by God: 'Moreover, the Father judges no one, but has entrusted all judgement to the Son' (John 5:22). This, among other things, Jesus acquires by virtue of his divine sonship. The Father works, so the Son works. The Father is honoured, so the Son is honoured. The Father has life in himself, so also has the Son. But it is specifically as Son of Man that Jesus inherits the right to judge: 'For as the Father has life in himself, so he has granted the Son to have life in himself. And he has given him authority to judge because he is the Son of Man' (John 5:26-27). The judge-like figure of the Son of Man in Daniel, the personal way in which Jesus applied the title Son of Man to himself and the teaching given by Jesus to his disciples about the Son of Man coming in his Father's glory with the holy angels all show how vital Jesus viewed his role as Judge to be.

The apostles confirm this application of the function of judgement to Christ. Peter at Cornelius' home and Paul in Athens both declare that God has appointed Christ to judge (Acts 10:42; 17:31). As an integral part of his gospel, Paul warns Christians at Rome of a day when God will judge men's secrets through Jesus Christ and confirms that we shall all stand before God's judgement seat by quoting from Isaiah:

"'As surely as I live," says the Lord,
"Every knee will bow before me;
    every tongue will confess to God'"
(Rom. 14:11; cf. Isa. 49:18; 45:23).

This latter passage (Isa. 45:23) Paul elsewhere refers to Christ in his judicial lordship (Phil. 2:11), so that he obviously sees no distinction between the judgement seat of God and that of Christ. It is rather a case of God delegating the function of judgement to Christ. Hence, Paul warns the Christians at Corinth in the same way: 'For we must all appear before the judgement seat of Christ, that each one may receive what is due to him for the things done while in the body, whether good or bad' (2 Cor. 5:10). The apostles accepted Jesus' right to act as judge of both living and dead.

The features of his ministry

Isaiah's Messiah is a just judge who exercises justice on a basis greater than that of human sagacity: 'He will not judge by what he sees with his eyes, or decide by what he hears with his ears' (Isa. 11:3). The normal means of obtaining a legal ruling through the senses of sight and hearing do not apply here. The verdict is reached by a higher process. This requires divine insight, for, while man judges by outward appearance, God assesses the heart (1 Sam. 16:7).

The reason for this divine insight, on which the Messiah's judgement is based, is given later: 'Righteousness will be his belt and faithfulness the sash round his waist' (Isa. 11:5). Practically, in the ancient Near East, the belt was an important piece of clothing. Its function was not simply to hold the garments together: it was used to tuck up long, flowing robes to allow vigorous, unimpeded activity. In this sense, it symbolizes completeness and efficiency. The belt was also an emblem of authority. Job speaks of God taking away the king's authority in terms of ungirding the belt (Job 12:18).

The comprehensive and effective nature of the Messiah's judging rests on his authority. Here the attributes of his divine character come into view. 'Righteousness' is his complete moral rectitude, his consistency with his own perfect standards. 'Faithfulness' is his covenant sureness based on his totally dependable character. This results in judgements of impartiality and equity. The anointing of Messiah's character by the Spirit extends to his judicial acts.

These same two features, penetrating insight and comprehensive judgement, mark Jesus' ministry. Together, they emphasize the fulfilment of this prophecy. The Gospel writers comment on the depth of Jesus' perception of the human heart. Faced by the violent opposition of enemies who claimed that Jesus was Beelzebub, the father of evil spirits, Matthew notes how Jesus knew their hearts and incisively rejected their reasoning (Matt. 12:25). Drawn by the apparent enthusiasm of an increasing number of new followers, John states how Jesus distanced himself from them, for he recognized their superficiality (John 2:25). Whether the scenario is criticism or adulation, Jesus penetrates to the truth with razor-like judgement and reaction.

It is in Jesus' own claims, however, that the comprehensiveness of his judgement and its divine standard are best seen. Confronted by those contesting the validity of his testimony Jesus replied, 'You judge by human standards; I pass judgement on no one. But if I do judge, my decisions are right, because I am not alone. I stand with the Father, who sent me. In your own Law it is written that the testimony of two men is valid. I am one who testifies for myself; my other witness is the Father, who sent me' (John 8:15-18).

Jesus relates the rightness of his judicial decisions to his unity with his Father. Earlier he attributed the justice of his judgements to the same source: 'By myself I can do nothing; I judge only as I hear, and my judgement is just, for I seek not to please myself but him who sent me' (John 5:30). It was as though the faculty of judgement was perfected by his oneness with his Father. The justice of Jesus' declarations emerges from his divine sonship. It is one of the attributes of the divine perfection of Jesus the Son of Man (John 5:27).

The righteousness and faithfulness which gird Isaiah's Christ find visible fulfilment in John's vision on Patmos. At the outset of his vision the one like a son of man has 'a golden sash round his chest' (Rev. 1:13). At the close of this revelation, the rider on the white horse, who exercises judgement and treads the winepress of the fury of God's wrath, is called Faithful and True (Rev. 19:11-15). The Son of Man, who in Daniel acts as a just judge before God on his people's behalf, in Revelation completes this mission in 'righteousness and faithfulness'.

The two aspects of judgement

Isaiah's Judge has a twofold task to perform — that of vindicating the righteous and condemning the wicked.

'But with righteousness he will judge the needy,
    with justice he will give decisions for the poor of the earth.

He will strike the earth with the rod of his mouth;
   with the breath of his lips he will slay the wicked'

(Isa. 11:4).

Isaiah describes in detail both the way in which the Judge carries out this work and the character of those receiving judgement. In regard to the righteous, he is said to judge with righteousness, that is, he is active in championing their cause and defending them. He also gives decisions for them — that is, he officially returns a verdict in their favour. As far as the wicked are concerned, he strikes them down in defeat and eventually destroys them. There is an immediacy about the implementing of his judgements. The agency through which he accomplishes this is his word, his legal pronouncements of condemnation, 'the rod of his mouth', 'the breath of his lips'.

The righteous are described firstly as 'needy', then as 'poor'. 'Needy' implies not only abject circumstances, but an awareness of these. 'Poor' is a further development of this. It means such an awareness of need that there is humility of spirit, meekness, a sense of hopelessness in one's own resources and strength. The wicked are described as 'the earth'. They are obviously different from 'the poor of the earth'. 'The earth' is the generality of mankind, godless and earthly-minded in attitude.

The fulfilment of these prophecies in Christ is clear. Jesus describes the 'blessed' condition of those in his kingdom. This blessedness is not mere human happiness, but the well-being of those under God's rule and consequently in a proper relationship with God. Specifically Jesus mentions those 'poor in spirit' (Matt. 5:3). His verdict of blessing rests on those who recognize their total lack of inner resource and declare their need. He speaks of the 'meek' as inheriting 'the earth' (Matt. 5:5). His pronouncement of true satisfaction is for those who reflect this poverty of spirit in an attitude of humility. He then promises vindication for those persecuted because of righteousness — theirs is the kingdom with its future reward. The declarations of the Messianic Judge are in total favour of his people. Whatever their outward circumstances, he pronounces blessing on them.

The condemnation of the wicked by Jesus' word as judge is equally forceful and immediate. Paul writes of the Lord Jesus overthrowing the lawless one by the breath of his mouth, quoting directly from Isaiah (2 Thess. 2:8).

At the beginning and end of his vision on Patmos, John sees a sharp sword of judgement coming from the mouth of the glorified Christ (Rev. 1:16; 19:15). Of this Homer Hailey writes, 'The "sword of his mouth" in John's writing is *the rod of His mouth* of Isaiah. It is by the rod of the Branch's mouth, the sword that proceeds out of His mouth, that He rules the nations and smites them in judgement. What Isaiah saw in prophetic vision of the future, John saw in vision as fulfilled in the present.'

These two functions of the Messianic Judge's work, vindication and condemnation, are closely related. They are like two sides of the one coin. 'The love that draws us near to him is hot with wrath to them.' This dual feature appears in the ministry of Jesus in a remarkable way. Just as Jesus, the promised Prince of Peace, when he came, brought not peace, but a sword, so Jesus, the Messianic Judge, at one time claims to judge and at another to desist from judging the world to which his Father had sent him. 'Jesus said, "For judgement I have come into this world, so that the blind will see and those who see will become blind"' (John 9:39). But he also said, 'As for the person who hears my words but does not keep them, I do not judge him. For I did not come to judge the world, but to save it' (John 12:47).

What is the resolution of this paradox, or apparent contradiction? I well remember as a boy singing that little chorus and feeling even then the difficulty:

> He did not come to judge the world,
> He did not come to blame,
> He did not only come to seek,
> It was to save he came.
> And when we call him Saviour,
> We call him by his name.

This chorus expresses an important biblical truth: namely, that Jesus' primary purpose, as his name implies, was to seek and save a lost world. In this sense, it expresses the teaching of John 12:47. What we must not suppose, however, is that judgement, in an absolute sense, was absent from Jesus' ministry. Jesus certainly did not mean that. Indeed, the very context in which Jesus' saving work is carried out is that of judgement. He vindicates the sinner in salvation; he judges those who reject him in condemnation. This is why Jesus claims that judgement has already come on the world. Whoever has the Son has life. Whoever has not the Son is condemned already (John 3:18).

Jesus confirms this dual aspect of judgement in one other area of his teaching. After his triumphal entry into Jerusalem and prior to his crucifixion, Jesus taught in the temple area. The focus of this teaching was a condemnation of the Jewish religious leaders. In the parable of the tenants Jesus quoted from Psalm 118 the words:

'The stone the builders rejected
  has become the capstone;
the Lord has done this,
  and it is marvellous in our eyes'

                    (Matt. 21:42; cf. Ps. 118:22-23),

and implied in his explanation that he as Messiah is the cornerstone.
Those who accept him are built upon this stone. Those who reject him
are crushed by it. Jesus as Messianic Judge both saves his people and
destroys his enemies. There are only the two alternatives. He is either
Saviour or Judge. He either acquits in mercy, or condemns in wrath.
This he does by virtue of his office as Judge.

The Son of Man

One final feature is worth noting. As sole and exclusive Judge, Jesus
fulfils the role of Daniel's Son of Man. In this double activity of
vindication and condemnation it is the same. The Son of Man who in
Daniel champions the saints before God and destroys God's enemies is
the Son of Man whom John sees on Patmos, the same who ultimately
delivers the saints and destroys the wicked.

The truth that Jesus is Judge has important implications. Too often
we preach a gospel of Jesus the loving Saviour without complementing
this truth with the terror of Jesus the wrathful Judge. Consequently, folk
hear the gospel with ease, discuss the possibility of following Jesus
abstractly and know nothing of a fearful looking to Christ for salvation.
The terror of the Lord is absent, for the Jesus we proclaim is Saviour
only, not Saviour and Judge. Neutrality still exists as a possible
response to our gospel. In reality, Scripture implies there are only two
choices. We find Christ as Saviour or face him as Judge. Either we
possess life, or already we stand condemned. There is, in addition, no
sense of urgency either in much modern evangelism. The final
judgement becomes a distant prospect. The Judge no longer stands at
the door.

When we recover the vision of Isaiah's Christ, a King whose rule
is successful, but who requires our obedience, a Messiah, anointed by
the Spirit, who looks for the reality of the fruit of the Spirit in our lives,
a Judge whose declarations are just, before whom we stand either
acquitted or condemned, we begin to see not only the glory of the Lord's
Christ but to face the challenge of his kingship. The burning vision of
Isaiah's Christ fulfilled in the Son of Man moves us in this direction. We
know better the nature of Christ the King and the kingdom over which
he rules.

3.
The salvation of Christ

The scene of prophecy changes dramatically in Isaiah 40. Hezekiah, King of Judah, had just told Isaiah how envoys from Babylon had come to visit him and how he had shown them all the treasures of his kingdom. Isaiah warned the king that these Babylonians would, in the future, sack the royal palace, carry off the treasures to Babylon and some of Hezekiah's own descendants would go into exile there. Hezekiah, however, was greatly relieved. God, who had spared him from death during illness, would now spare him the disgrace and defeat of Babylonian exile. '"The word of the Lord you have spoken is good," Hezekiah replied. For he thought, "There will be peace and security in my lifetime"' (Isa. 39:8).

The next oracle is one of hope. It speaks of God comforting his people. Days of hardship are past. Israel's sins are forgiven. God has restored Jerusalem. Zion is to broadcast that message far and wide. The sovereign Lord has come with power. God's glory has been revealed (Isa. 40:1-11). This is clearly a different era. The scenario is no longer the threatening advances of Babylon, nor even the dreary days of exile there. It seems, rather, to be a time towards the end of the exile when hope abounded. Cyrus, the Persian king, appeared at that time in a strange way, as the Lord's messiah, the means of breaking Babylonian power and of ensuring the return of the Jews to their homeland.

Indeed, hope is the major theme of Isaiah's continuing predictions. Liberation is in the air. Isaiah chapters 40-48 promise brighter days ahead. Hope, fitfully expressed by the prophet in the past, now becomes his consuming passion, a word burning within him which he must proclaim. The message of Isaiah 40:1-11 predicts Christ's salvation. It forecasts a greater deliverance than that from Babylonian captivity. It announces ultimately God's redemption of his people from sin through

Christ the Messiah. The new exodus from Babylon is only a token of
the salvation which Christ eventually brings. The means by which
Christ will accomplish this is also foretold. He will act as Prophet,
Priest and King for his people.

Priest

The opening words of the prophecy predict the priestly aspect of
Christ's salvation.

> 'Comfort, comfort my people,
>   says your God.
> Speak tenderly to Jerusalem,
>   and proclaim to her
> that her hard service has been completed,
>   that her sin has been paid for,
> that she has received from the Lord's hand
>   double for all her sins'

(Isa. 40:1-2).

God comforts his people

There is a tenderness about this comfort which is surprisingly new and
fresh. Isaiah had previously brought some light into Judah's darkness,
but these were isolated occurrences. Mostly his words were of doom
and gloom. Prophecies and woes against the surrounding nations,
Babylon, Damascus, Tyre and Egypt, were coupled with stern
judgements against Judah and Jerusalem. The prophets were all alike
in that. Amos condemned social injustice. Jeremiah exposed prevalent
idolatry. Hosea berated a lack of love and obedience towards God.
Zechariah predicted the day of God's judgement. Here, Isaiah turns in
tenderness to console God's people. He had already called the people,
in God's name, to come and reason with God so that their sin might be
cleansed (Isa. 1:18).

The very word 'comfort' stresses this. It means literally 'to cause to
breathe again'. There is a reviving and renewing aspect about God's
comfort to help his people in their distress. It not only relieves their
situation but brings hope and new life to them in their despair. They start
living again. It is a comfort directed 'to the heart', which the NIV rightly
renders 'tenderly'. There is nothing superficial about God's help. It
addresses the problem and assists at the point of need. But it does this
lovingly. The expression combines ideas both of reassurance and

sympathy. It speaks of winning a person back. Both Joseph and Hosea spoke 'to the heart'. Joseph's words inspired his brothers with confidence in their fearfulness in Egypt (Gen. 50:21). Hosea's tender advances to his faithless wife Gomer were aimed at restoration, not at the condemnation she deserved (Hosea 2:14-16). God through Isaiah reassures his people at the deepest level of intimacy and offers them hope amid their distress. In this way, God wins them back to himself.

The comfort is also complete. The first words of the prophecy are God's command not just to one prophet, but to many. A whole chorus of prophetic voices is to convey God's consolation to his people. There must be no possibility of their missing the message. It is repeated so that they will know how determined God is in his desire to help them. The details of this comfort are totally reassuring. Three metaphors drive it home effectively. Taking the picture from the battlefield, their time of military service has been completed. In terms of commerce, their sin has been paid off. In the court of God's justice, they have been thoroughly punished for their crimes. All their sufferings are past. The days of darkness are over. Not only that, but any wrongs they have perpetrated during that period have been more than adequately dealt with. The debt of the past has been settled and there is bright hope for the future. There is a comprehensiveness about God's comfort.

The tenderness of a priest

What is the connection, however, between this prophetic word of comfort in Isaiah and the priestly office of Christ? Are there any grounds for seeing in embryo here in Isaiah what came to fulfilment in Jesus' priesthood? The link is the tenderness of God's comfort which deals effectively with his people's sins. The word to Judah's 'heart' was that hardship was over because sin had been paid for and punishment for sin doubly meted out.

In Old Testament times the priests, assisted by the Levites, carried out the functions of worship in general and the offering of sacrifice in particular. The offering of sacrifice was God's prescribed way of 'atoning for', or covering over sin. In this, the priests and Levites were expected both to be meticulous in outer ceremonial and to live moral lives so that they might deal justly and gently with those among God's people who were straying. They were to show tenderness and sympathy, avoiding crass indifference on the one hand and unjust sentimentality on the other.

Moses and Aaron were exemplary in this. Under constant provocation they dealt patiently with the wrongs of the Israelites. They restrained a craving among the people to return to Egypt and successfully defused a rebellion among the Levites. They did this by praying to God to avert his wrath from the people. On one remarkable occasion Aaron ran with the priest's censer in his hand among the plague-ridden people. He stood between the living and the dead, and the plague stopped (Num. 16:46-50). The sympathetic intervention of the priest was the instrument through which God's comforting atonement reached his people. This is the connection between the comfort proclaimed by Isaiah to the Jews and the priesthood of Christ.

The letter to the Hebrews expounds the priesthood of Christ. It shows how all the Old Testament prophecies of a Messianic Priest were fulfilled in Jesus. It stresses, too, the tenderness of Jesus as Priest and the effectiveness of his priestly work. On both scores, it relates to the comfort Isaiah proclaimed.

In Hebrews the tenderness of Christ the Priest is seen in his humanity. Christ assumes not the nature of angels, but the seed of Abraham. He takes to himself flesh and blood. This humanity is not just apparent but real. Christ is truly man. He faced adversity from the devil, for he was tempted in all points as we are, yet never sinned. He experienced limitations in his human existence, for he learned through what he suffered. He expressed human dependence and emotion. He prayed with tears and strong crying. It is because of this oneness with mankind that he can sympathize with and help those who are in trouble. Through his humanity he is a tender and understanding comforter. The Gospel stories recall Christ's humanity in the most vivid way. Jesus suffers loneliness, misunderstanding, sorrow, grief, rejection, desertion, hunger and pain. In all of this he is our fellow-sufferer and can offer us succour and comfort. This is the background against which Hebrews affirms the intercessory work of Christ.

The perfect sacrifice of Christ

The effectiveness of Christ's priestly work in Hebrews is traced to his divine nature as Son of God. Christ is both priest and victim. The sacrifice he offers is perfect in God's sight. It is perfect because it is personal. It is a self-sacrifice. He offers himself up in sinless purity to God. Christ's own blood, not the blood of animals, constitutes the sacrifice. The animal offerings of Old Testament days provided ceremonial cleansing.

Christ's sacrifice purges the conscience from dead works to serve the living God. Christ offers himself in the proper setting — not the temple in Jerusalem, but heaven itself. In that sense, the temple sacrifices were the mere shadow of which Christ's offering is the fulfilment, the reality. Christ's sacrifice is perfect because it is final. No further sacrifice for sin is needed. Christ sets aside all the older forms of sacrifice that he might establish his own sacrifice. He offered himself once for all. His work completed, he sat down at God's right hand, the place of privilege and power. He is a priest of a higher order than that of Levi. His priesthood is conferred by God, not man. He is of the priestly line of Melchizedek. Hence, his sacrifice is the culmination of all former sacrifices while making subsequent sacrifices unnecessary.

Christ's sacrifice makes the worshipper perfect for ever. The comfort which it offers is complete and effective. 'Christ executeth the office of a priest, in his once offering himself a sacrifice without spot to God, to be a reconciliation for the sins of his people; and in making continual intercession for them' (*Larger Catechism,* 44).

The priesthood of Christ in Hebrews

The tenderness and effectiveness of Christ's comfort as Priest are not just evident generally in the letter to the Hebrews, but particularly in reference to Isaiah. Hebrews 2:5-14 expounds Christ's humanity. It emphasizes how, as a merciful and faithful High Priest, Christ not only helps those who are tempted, but makes atonement for the sins of the people. In the course of his explanation the writer quotes from the Old Testament. Making the point that God subjects the world to come not to angels but men, he quotes from Psalm 8:

'What is man that you are mindful of him,
   the son of man that you care for him?
You made him a little lower than the angels;
   you crowned him with glory and honour
   and put everything under his feet'

(Heb. 2:6-8; cf. Ps. 8:4-6).

The writer has in mind Jesus 'made a little lower than the angels' (Heb. 2:9).

Jesus, in leading many sons to glory as the pioneer of their salvation, identifies unashamedly with them as brothers. To drive this point home, the writer quotes from Psalm 22 and Isaiah 8:

'He says,

   "I will declare your name to my brothers;
      in the presence of the congregation I will sing your praises."

And again,

"I will put my trust in him."

And again he says,

"Here am I, and the children God has given me"'
                                    (Heb. 2:12-13; cf. Ps. 22:22; Isa. 8:17-18).

Psalm 22 is clearly Messianic if for no other reason than that Jesus
spoke its opening words from the cross. The allusion to Isaiah 8 is more
difficult to understand, but the context helps. Isaiah, frustrated by a lack
of response to his prophecies of deliverance, urges his disciples to seal
up his sayings. He will wait for the Lord, who is hiding his face from
the house of Jacob. He will put his trust in God (Isa. 8:16-17). The
quotation of Isaiah 8:17 reflects the same faith on the part of Isaiah as
David showed in Psalm 22. Although at this moment left an orphan by
God, David is sure that God will not always hide his face from him. The
day will come when, troubles over, he will praise God's name openly
among his brothers (Ps. 22:1, 22-24). The identification will be one of
great comfort and open victory.

Isaiah 8:18 is quoted separately. This shows that it stresses
something distinct. Isaiah's family are symbols for Israel: 'Here am I,
and the children the Lord has given me. We are signs and symbols in
Israel from the Lord Almighty, who dwells on Mount Zion' (Isa. 8:18).
The names of Isaiah's two sons were Shear-Jashub, meaning 'Remnant
will return', and Maher-Shalal-Hash-Baz, meaning 'Hasten booty,
speed spoil'. Isaiah's own name meant 'Jehovah is salvation'. Aware
of the difficulties involved in his mission, Isaiah was still confident of
ultimate triumph. Indeed, a remnant from the exiled people would
return to give proof of God's victory in salvation. God had reminded
Isaiah of this when he had called him as prophet and his sons' names
confirmed this to him.

The promise of a Messianic community in Isaiah 8 leads to the
prediction of the Messianic King of Isaiah 9. Isaiah 40 takes up this
hopeful strain and develops the comfort this salvation brings as it
heralds the return from exile. The identification of the Messiah with his
people is an integral part of the whole process. It is through him and his
oneness with his people that the tender and effective comfort of
salvation comes. The writer to the Hebrews stresses this solidarity as he
quotes from Isaiah.

Of these three quotations P. E. Hughes writes, 'The messianic
application of these three texts, then, lends support to our author's

doctrine that the incarnate Son is one in humanity with those whom he redeems and whom he calls brothers, the first describing the effectual communication by the triumphant Saviour of the redemption he has achieved to his brethren, the second emphasizing the fellow-dependence on God of him who is the sharer of our humanity, and the third declaring the sovereignty of God who by his act of grace in Christ makes us his children (cf. John 1:12) and gives us as brethren to his Son.'

The humanity of Christ

The humanity of Christ the Priest is the means whereby his comfort identifies with us. The purpose behind this identification is atonement, the forgiveness of our sins. In this, he is our pioneer and leader, who not only rescues us from sin and helps us in temptation, but forms us into a community of his children whom he leads from grace to glory. Truly, he is unashamed to call us brothers. God's comfort speaks to our hearts, deals effectively in forgiving our sins and constitutes us a community of forgiven people, the church.

The humanity of Christ needs constantly to be stressed. It is particularly easy to undervalue this aspect of our Lord's nature. The divinity of Christ, so clearly taught in Scripture, can lead to the assumption that Christ's was only the semblance of humanity. This is far from the case. The physical, emotional, intellectual and religious humanity of Jesus is written into the very fabric of the Gospel records. It is confirmed in the letters of the New Testament. Yet this never conflicts with the clear portrayal of Christ's divinity. The two natures stand side by side miraculously and mysteriously, the one doing no harm to the other. Christ is both truly human and truly divine.

The humanity of Christ brings great comfort. Christ stands alongside his people in all of life's varying experiences, empathizing with them, for he shares their nature. He was tempted in all points like they are, yet without sin. The Scottish paraphrase puts this well:

Where high the heavenly temple stands,
The house of God not made with hands,
A great High Priest our nature wears,
The guardian of mankind appears.

He who for men their surety stood,
And poured on earth his precious blood,
Pursues in heaven his mighty plan,
The Saviour and the friend of man.

Though now ascended up on high,
He bends on earth a brother's eye;
Partaker of the human name,
He knows the frailty of our frame.

Our fellow-sufferer yet retains
A fellow-feeling of our pains;
And still remembers in the skies
His tears, his agonies, and cries.

In every pang that rends the heart,
The Man of sorrows has a part;
He sympathizes with our grief,
And to the sufferer sends relief.

With boldness, therefore, at the throne,
Let us make all our sorrows known;
And ask the aids of heavenly power
To help us in the evil hour.

The purpose of Christ's humanity can, however, be misrepresented. The comfort is directed to our condition as creatures. But, above all, it deals with the fallenness of that condition. Like the comfort of Isaiah's prophecy, it relates primarily to forgiveness of sins. It is not just sympathy, but saving sympathy.

The apostles make this purpose clear as they spell out the implications of Jesus' humanity. The writer to the Hebrews recalls how Christ assumed flesh and blood that he might not only sympathize with man, but ultimately destroy the devil, deliver those in fear of death from their bondage and provide atonement for sin (Heb. 2:14-18). Paul reminds his readers that Christ came in the likeness of sinful flesh to be a 'sin offering' (Rom. 8:3). John describes the Word becoming flesh so that man might receive Christ and be born of God (John 1:12-14). The true intent of Christ's comfort is salvation from sin.

The same saving comfort marks Jesus' own ministry. Christ calls those burdened by sin to come to him for rest (Matt.11:28-30). He bids those thirsting for life to drink of him (John 7:37-38). Christ is the Good Shepherd who not only knows his sheep intimately, but dies for them (John 10:14-15). He does not leave his disciples orphaned but sends them another Comforter, the Holy Spirit, one like himself, who will reprove the world of sin and lead his followers into truth (John 14:16-17; 16:12-13).

Isaiah's comfort, directed towards the relief of God's people in their bitter distress in exile, finds ultimate fulfilment in Christ. Christ the High Priest not only identifies with his people, but atones for their sins. This understanding must inform our presentation of salvation. The warmth of a message to the heart and the effectiveness of a gospel of redemption from sin are the features of Christ's salvation which call for emphasis in our evangelism today. This alone will win a lost world for Christ and ensure a continued growth in grace. It is Isaiah who prophetically recalls us to this task.

King

Isaiah prophesies Christ the King:

> 'A voice of one calling:
> "In the desert prepare
>   the way for the Lord;
> make straight in the wilderness
>   a highway for our God.
> Every valley shall be raised up,
>   every mountain and hill made low;
> the rough ground shall become level,
>   the rugged places a plain.
> And the glory of the Lord will be revealed,
>   and all mankind together will see it.
> > For the mouth of the Lord has spoken"'
> > (Isa. 40:3-5).

The comfort Isaiah has been speaking about comes from God. God will come like a mighty King and lead his people from exile to their homeland. Because God is King, preparations have to be made. Those preparations require change. As on the human level a royal visit involves extensive preparations, so much more the coming of God as King. God's greatness demands this.

The glory of God

The majesty of God as King pervades Isaiah's oracle at this point. The chorus of prophetic voices proclaiming comfort gives way to one lone voice, a voice calling. The voice is nameless and nondescript, for as a person he is unimportant. His only function is to communicate. He acts as the herald of a king, the outrider of a commander-in-chief. The voice cries about the glory of God. God's glory will be disclosed and all people will see it. God confirms this fact by word of mouth. There could be no more important message than that of the glory of God. The glory of God is the outshining of his greatness. The Hebrew word for glory, *kabod,* means literally 'weight' or 'heaviness'. It speaks of the imposing and impressive nature of God's being. In the Bible, God's glory describes his presence among mankind often in some majestic or extraordinary setting, a cloud or earthquake, a supernatural, visible manifestation of God.

Moses experienced the glory of God. The cloud on Sinai hid God's glory from the people. The cloud by day and the fiery glow by night over the Israelite camp were visible tokens of the divine presence. When Moses went to the tabernacle, he was said to speak with God 'face to face'. Yet all recognized that to gaze on the full glory of God would mean death. So, while Moses prayed to see God's glory, it was only partly disclosed to him, as he stood hidden in the cleft of the rock (Exod. 33:7-23). The glory of God continued to rest on the tabernacle and, in time, on the temple.

Ezekiel too had a remarkable vision of the glory of God. Among the exiles beside the Kebar river he saw that strange sight of the wheeled creatures beneath the throne of God (Ezek. 1:1-28). He saw the same vision departing out of the temple into the desert lands of the east and returning from that direction at a later time (Ezek. 10:1-22; 43:1-5). In this way Ezekiel experienced the departure of God's glory from Jerusalem during the captivity and rejoiced in its return at the close of the exile.

Isaiah's experience of God's glory was similar to that of Ezekiel. At the outset of his prophetic ministry Isaiah encountered God's glory in the temple (Isa. 6:1-13). The occasion was significant. It was the year of King Uzziah's death. The relative peace and prosperity of his stable reign were over. Isaiah was encouraged to know that, while the human king had departed, the glory of the divine King remained with his people. This vision challenged Isaiah to respond to God's call.

Like Ezekiel, Isaiah recognized the absence of the divine glory during the exile. Here, in chapter 40, he offers words of great comfort as he depicts the return of God's glory. Not only those in the temple but all mankind will see this glory. The voice, then, in the trackless desert, heralds the revelation of God's glory. Isaiah predicts a day when the exile will end. God will comfort his people by coming to them and disclosing to them his greatness. God himself will lead them from captivity to the homeland. Because of this, preparations must be made. Changes are required to welcome the King. These changes are all the more necessary, for it is the glory of the Lord which is to be revealed. The preparations must be worthy of such a disclosure.

Preparing the way

The changes must be absolute, too. This is clear as the oracle continues. Valleys are to be raised, mountains lowered, rough ground levelled, rugged terrain is to become a plain. In each case, an exactly opposite condition from the present one is envisaged. While the words are a general description for a clearing through the oriental wasteland, this feature is basic. A complete reversal of the existing situation is in mind. Every barrier to the King's coming must be removed. Even in the metaphor of landscape this will involve dramatic changes of a fundamental nature to the current scene.

Charles and Norma Ellis recall the achievements of pioneers in their own homeland in this connection: 'As we think of the early settlers in our own country struggling to ford rivers and cross mountains in their westward trek across the American continent, and then think of the valleys now filled in and the mountains now levelled or tunnelled through to accommodate super-highways, we have a graphic picture of the way preparation was made for the glory of the Lord to be revealed among men.'

Changes of this nature can be quite remarkable. The area where I lived as a boy was between two small provincial towns. Forward planning designed to twin these into a large city complex. The plan, to some extent, misfired and the work was not entirely successful. However, sufficient changes were made to the countryside that, when I revisit it, I find myself confused about known landmarks and even, at times, get lost. Some roads have become dead-ends. Others were widened and reshaped. Yet others have disappeared, buried under tons of earth. Even the piecemeal changes make a startling difference.

Isaiah's prophecy calls for radical change. While the details might be pressed too far, that much is clear. Internal and external obstacles must be removed in preparation for the coming of the King. The overall challenge of the prophet's words recalls the Bible's call to repentance, especially in the Old Testament expression *sub*, which means a complete 'about-turn'. F. Delitzsch details this change: 'The command, according to its spiritual interpretation, points to the encouragement of those who are cast down, the humiliation of the self-righteous and self-secure, the changing of dishonesty into simplicity, and of unapproachable haughtiness into submission... In general, the meaning is that Israel is to take care, that the God who is coming to deliver it shall find it in such an outward and inner state as befits His exaltation and His purpose.'

There is another side to the prophet's words which is sometimes overlooked. The call is not only a command requiring man's repentance and obedience, but a promise revealing God's grace. The preparation is both a human responsibility and a divine gift. Calvin comments on the phrase, 'Every valley shall be raised up', like this: 'These words might with propriety be rendered in the imperative mood, "Let every valley be exalted," so as to be placed in immediate connection with the command which God gives by his prophets to prepare and level the way for himself; but it makes hardly any difference in the meaning. Let us be satisfied with understanding the prophet's design, "that, although many and formidable difficulties are started to hinder the salvation of the Church, still the hand of God will be victorious and will prevail".' God not only requires change; he initiates it. Isaiah's prophecy here may well have this meaning, for it agrees with other statements he makes on the same subject.

Isaiah alludes elsewhere to a highway that God will provide for his people. He predicts that a road would be opened up for the remnant to return from Assyria, just as Israel came up from Egypt (Isa. 11:16). Indeed, a way would run from Egypt to Assyria extending God's blessings beyond the Jews to their two captors (Isa. 19:23). In the transformation of the land accompanying Israel's restoration, Isaiah promised the exiles a highway called the 'Way of Holiness' (Isa. 35:8-10). Elsewhere he speaks of God turning mountains into roads, raising up highways and clearing boulders so that not only Israel but other nations might benefit from God's goodness (Isa. 49:11; 62:10). He depicts God providing a highway for his people and removing all obstacles before them. The highway of Isaiah 40 is also for the benefit of God's people. God comes to reveal his glory among them, but the practical outworking of this is in their return from Babylonian exile. What need has the omnipotent God of a road, but for the feet of his own people? No barrier will impede their progress. God himself will ensure that.

The coming of John the Baptist foretold

Isaiah's prophecy of the preparations for the coming Messianic King was fulfilled in the life and ministry of John the Baptist. All the Gospel writers make this clear. Matthew, Mark and Luke quote this passage from Isaiah directly (Matt. 3:3; Mark 1:3; Luke 3:4-6) and John alludes to it (John 1:19-28).

As with Isaiah, the Gospels stress the overriding importance of the coming Messiah. John the Baptist claims that, while he baptizes with water, one is coming who will baptize with the Holy Spirit. John is inferior to this coming one. He is unworthy even to loose the thong of his sandals. The Messiah will come after John in time, but is preferred far above him in rank. Questioned by a deputation of Jewish leaders, John categorically denies that he is the Christ, Elijah or 'the Prophet'. He describes himself simply as 'the voice of one calling in the desert, "Make straight the way for the Lord"' (John 1:23). The desert location, John's clothing and diet all confirm his vocation. John regarded himself as the voice of Isaiah 40:3.

Preparation was the keynote of John's message. It was summed up in his peremptory command: 'Repent for the kingdom of heaven is near' (Matt. 3:2). John's baptism was a baptism of repentance for forgiveness of sins. The entire thrust of his work was that people should prepare for the Messiah's coming by turning from sin to God for forgiveness. They were to produce fruit worthy of repentance. They must give evidence of a real sorrow for sin by turning from it to be ready for the King when he arrives.

John, like Isaiah, demanded absolute change (Luke 3:7-14). The turning involved in repentance was not to be superficial but real. Those coming to his baptism asked what they were to do. John told them that people who had two tunics should share with those who had none. Those who had food should do the same. Tax collectors were urged to exact no more than was required. Soldiers were neither to extort money nor accuse people falsely. They were also to be content with their pay. All this was solidly grounded in reality. It had to do with the practicalities of daily life. It involved radical decisions resulting in new attitudes and a different lifestyle. People did not normally share their possessions like that. Tax collectors were known for their exorbitant demands. Soldiers abused their position of authority to the detriment of the people. Repentance meant a right about-turn in every sense of the word. Mountains must be flattened, valleys filled in, the crooked straightened, the rough smoothed out.

In a strange way these changes, while they placed an obligation on his hearers, were ultimately God's doing. John's preaching was successful (Matt. 3:5-12). The whole Judean countryside, along with all the people of Jerusalem, came to him and, confessing their sins, were baptized in the Jordan. Even scribes and Pharisees came to John. 'Who has warned you to come scuttling out of the undergrowth like a brood of snakes?' he asks. God's hand was in this. The axe was laid at the root of the tree. They must be careful that their interest is genuine and their repentance true. God needs neither them, nor their deference to John, nor their religious background. God could raise up children for Abraham from the stones lying around them. Indeed, any sincere aspirations of repentance they profess to have must come from God, like fruit from a tree. Fruitless branches are consigned to the fire. Good fruit must be the worthwhile evidence of the change which repentance requires.

John's success continued (John 3:22-35). Folk constantly came to be baptized by him at Aenon near Salim. John's disciples, in dispute with a certain Jew, were reminded by their teacher of his inferiority to the Messiah. John was the best man, but Jesus the bridegroom. John must decrease and Jesus increase. It mattered little that the Pharisees heard how Jesus' disciples were baptizing more people than John. It was only proof of progress. God was behind both John and Jesus in their work. The end of all this process was the disclosure of God's glory. Isaiah had predicted that. God brought this about through John's ministry of preparation. Luke, conscious that the gospel was not only for Jews but also for Gentiles, quotes most extensively of all the Gospel writers from Isaiah 40 at this point. He closes his quotation with the words: 'And all mankind will see God's salvation' (Luke 3:6). The glory of God is his salvation. That salvation is revealed in Jesus the Messiah.

John, in his Gospel, drives this point home. John the Baptist is a man sent from God to witness to the coming light. John was a burning and shining lamp; Jesus is the uncreated light. John is the human herald, Jesus the divine Word. 'The Word became flesh and made his dwelling among us. We have seen his glory, the glory of the One and Only [Son], who came from the Father, full of grace and truth' (John 1:14).

The call to repentance

The preaching of the gospel of the kingdom must include the demand for repentance. This note is sadly lacking in much of today's evangelism. We are shown the beauty of Jesus, the attractiveness of the gospel and the excitement of change which following Jesus brings. All these are legitimate ingredients. But the necessary factor of repentance from sin is glaringly absent. Under this regime, conversion is a relatively easy matter. It involves simply a decision for Jesus where the emphasis is on the human action of receiving Christ, but little is said about the change in attitude necessary for such a reception. Sin is not emphasized. Hence, no effective barrier exists to such a reception. There is no consciousness of sin and its effects in the human heart and, consequently, no awareness that our nature is sinful and the pathway to God obstructed. This is an easy salvation.

The rugged cry of Isaiah's voice fulfilled in the Baptist's summons to 'repent' needs to be heard again. We must start from this point if we are truly to present a gospel which involves repentance towards God and faith in the Lord Jesus (Acts 20:21). The Puritans have much to teach us here. Their constant 'law preaching' brought the terror of God's standards before their hearers and left them in little doubt as to their sinful condition. Man must again tremble under the rigours of God's demands in Scripture if we are to experience anything of the Spirit's work of convincing a world of sin and to see that world savingly converted to Christ.

The gospel of repentance must not simply be addressed to the emotions. Feelings are involved, but true repentance is much more than feeling sorry, or even being sorry. It involves change, complete and radical change, at the deepest level of human existence. It is essentially an about-turn in our attitude towards God, ourselves and our sin. That is why demands for repentance must be addressed to the will. Isaiah and John the Baptist are at one in this. The relevance of the challenge to turn in sorrow from sin to God will be evident in the fruit which results from a changed life. The *Shorter Catechism* describes this aspect when it claims that 'repentance unto life' means turning from sin to God 'with full purpose of, and endeavour after, new obedience' (*Shorter Catechism,* 87). Changed attitudes and lives are the worthy fruit of this. There will be a complete reversal of former patterns of behaviour. True repentance will produce fruit in character and daily living.

The change involved in repentance, while a human responsibility, is also the gift of God. God himself comes and removes all barriers to his people's progress. There are dangers to be avoided in a wrongful 'preparationism'. Any suggestion that by repentance we merit or earn God's favour is wrong. The idea, too, that repentance is a kind of probationary period which, when successfully completed, opens the door of the kingdom, is equally dangerous. The fact that many reformed confessions in their 'order of salvation' place repentance after faith makes that point clearly. God is the author of the change involved in repentance. While it comes as a human obligation of response to the Messianic King, God initiates it. God granted even to Gentiles repentance unto life (Acts 11:18). This fact does not detract from human responsibility. It underlines it as a glorious possibility.

As a King, Christ demands absolute obedience of those who are to be his subjects. This involves repentance as a complete turning from sin to God. Isaiah predicts this and John the Baptist's ministry fulfils it. The truly exciting thing about repentance, however, is that the God who demands this absolute about-turn also gives it. Such is the power of the kingly Messiah.

'Christ executeth the office of a king in subduing us to himself, in ruling and defending us and in restraining and conquering all his and our enemies' (*Shorter Catechism,* 26).

Prophet

Isaiah also foresees a Christ who is Prophet.

'A voice says, "Cry out."
    And I said, "What shall I cry?"

"All men are like grass,
    and all their glory is like the flowers of the field.
The grass withers and the flowers fall,
    because the breath of the Lord blows on them.
    Surely the people are grass.
The grass withers and the flowers fall,
    but the word of our God stands for ever."
You who bring good tidings to Zion,
    go up on a high mountain.
You who bring good tidings to Jerusalem,
    lift up your voice with a shout,
lift it up, do not be afraid;
    say to the towns of Judah
    "Here is your God!"
See, the Sovereign Lord comes with power,
    and his arm rules for him.
See, his reward is with him,
    and his recompense accompanies him.
He tends his flock like a shepherd:
    He gathers the lambs in his arms
and carries them close to his heart;
    he gently leads those that have young'

(Isa. 40:6-11).

The transience of man

A chorus of prophetic voices brings the comfort of the Priest. A lone
voice issues the command to prepare for the King. A loud, authoritative
voice introduces the message of the Prophet. The voice cries out. The
message is essentially about the finite nature of man and the eternity of
God. As Isaiah foresees God's people languishing in exile he is
conscious of their weakness and frailty. They are victims not only of
their Babylonian overlords, but of their own, innate helplessness. Grass
is the perfect metaphor to describe them. Grass, which quickly springs
up in the heat of the Middle East, suddenly withers and perishes.

Earlier, Isaiah spoke of God's destruction of Sennacherib's army in this way.

'They are like plants in the field,
    like tender green shoots,
like grass sprouting on the roof,
    scorched before it grows up'

(Isa. 37:27).

Here he claims that God's people share this transiency with all humanity. The flesh of man disintegrates before the Spirit, or breath, of Jehovah. H. C. Leupold expresses it well: 'Grass came out beautifully in spring in the Holy Land and after a few weeks withered and shrivelled. So is man with his human strength. It demands greater resources than these to build in a lasting way in the kingdom of God.'

Isaiah implies more than simply the frailty of human nature, however. The analogy is not simply that flesh is like grass, but that the glory of human nature is like the perishable flower. The Hebrew word translated 'glory' is *chesed*. It means, literally, 'grace' and denotes all that is naturally most highly valued among men. Isaiah claims that the best of man's glory, the flower of his nature, his achievements, success and finest accomplishments are all alike transient and perishable. This is because of sin. Man is not simply frail; he is also fallen, and he is frail because he is fallen. Calvin comments: 'The prophet seems, as if in mockery, to add a sort of correction; for *a flower* is something more than *grass*. It is, therefore, an acknowledgement, that, although men have some shining qualities, like flowers in the fields, yet the beauty and lustre quickly vanish and pass away, so that it is useless for them to flatter or applaud themselves on account of this idle and deceitful splendour.'

Moses recalled the same transiency in similar circumstances. He had led God's people for almost forty years in the desert. He had seen their rebellion against God, listened to their constant complaining, settled their internal disputes and realized that, in all this, they were being punished by God. At the end of that period of wandering, he reflects,

'You sweep men away in the sleep of death;
    they are like the new grass of the morning—
though in the morning it springs up new,
    by evening it is dry and withered'

(Ps. 90:5-6).

Moses knew that Israel's sin underlies their frailty. God turns men back to dust, consumes them in his anger, parades their secret sins before his very face and causes them to end their days under his wrath with a moan. Their only hope is that God will relent and have mercy on them, that he will reverse the whole sad process and make them glad for as many days as he has afflicted them.

The enduring Word of God

The answer to those aspirations and longings of Moses is found in Isaiah's message. 'But the word of our God stands for ever' (Isa. 40:8). The finiteness of man is resolved in the eternity of God. Man's frailty and fallenness find hope only in the forgiveness and renewal of God. The instrument through which this comes is God's Word. It alone remains amid all the changing sequences of human existence. The flesh of man is hopeless as the breath of God blows on it. The same breath, however, will blow in recreating grace. The Spirit of God will accomplish this transformation through the Word of God which stands for ever.

Isaiah directs the Jews to the enduring Word of God. The message of hope reaches a climax as he depicts a prophetess bringing good news to Jerusalem. News of victory in battle in Old Testament days was often spread by women. The prophetess 'evangelizes'. The Word of God is a gospel word. The Hebrew term translated 'bring good tidings' is *bissér*. F. Delitzsch writes, 'The verb *bissér* signifies literally to smooth, to unfold, then to make glad, more especially with joyful news.' God, through Isaiah's words, was smoothing over the rough experience of the years of exile with the glad news that he himself was coming to deliver his people from captivity.

The details of this news are even more inspiring. They recall the sovereignty of the King for whom Isaiah had required preparation and the tenderness of the Priest who would deal effectively with sin (Isa. 40:10,11). The King comes ruling with power, vindicating his own people with victory, recompensing their enemies with destruction. The Priest comes as a tender shepherd, leading not driving, carrying the young and comforting the weak. This gospel combines strength and tenderness, power and love, sovereignty and grace.

The good news is the enduring Word of God to a finite and flawed humanity. The one who communicates this message is the Prophet. The comfort of the Priest and the command of the King come through the word of the Prophet. Christ fulfils this particular work as the great Prophet of God. 'Christ executeth the office of a prophet, in his revealing to the church, in all ages, by his Spirit and word, in divers ways of administration, the whole will of God, in all things concerning their edification and salvation' (*Larger Catechism,* 43).

Isaiah's words were fulfilled in the New Testament in Peter's first letter. There were similarities between the situation which Isaiah addressed and that of the churches to whom Peter wrote. Peter describes his readers as God's scattered elect, Christians of the dispersion, exiled from their true homeland, expatriates in temporary residence on earth. Their lot was not an easy one. Christian slaves were being ill-treated by pagan masters. Christian wives were finding it difficult to live with non-Christian husbands. An alien and antagonistic world was pressing in on these small churches. They had had to suffer grief in all kinds of trials and their present prospects were particularly painful. In all of this, their frail nature and transient existence was fearfully to the fore. They were like the Jews in Babylon.

Peter's answer to their problem strikingly resembles Isaiah's message to the Jews. Peter proposes a gospel word to remedy their precarious position. In a world where they were insignificant and unimportant, Peter tells them that they are the object of God's choice and have been given a living hope (1 Peter 1:3). An eternal message from God will transform their depressing human circumstances. He reminds them that they have an abiding inheritance in heaven which is reserved for them, just as they are preserved for it (1 Peter 1:4-5). He recalls the prophetic word of deliverance through a Messiah, a word not primarily for the prophets in their day and generation but for Peter's readers, in their present distress (1 Peter 1:10-12). He assures them that they have been redeemed, not with perishable money, but with precious blood (1 Peter 1:18-19). They have been born again, not of corruptible seed, but of incorruptible, through the living and enduring Word of God. He then quotes Isaiah 40:6-8:

'For
"All men are like grass,
    and all their glory is like the flowers of the field;
the grass withers and the flowers fall,
    but the word of the Lord stands for ever"'

(1 Peter 1:24-25),

and concludes that this was the word that was preached to them. The eternal Word of God is the gospel word about Christ.

The parallels are inescapable: the hopeless human condition, the divine prophetic answer, the fulfilment in the coming Christ, the consequent regeneration of life and the instrumentality of the gospel message 'through the living and enduring word of God' (1 Peter 1:23).

Christ is both communicator and substance of the salvation he brings. He is the Prophet, Priest and King of his people.

The living Word and the written Word

The instrumentality of God's Word in salvation needs stressing today. A false division between Christ, the living Word, and Scripture, the written Word, unfortunately still persists. Christ and Scripture are wrongly wrested apart. I first met this when starting to study theology. The argument was put in this way: the Scriptures merely contain the word of God but must not be equated with the Word of God. To do this is to denigrate Christ, who alone is the Word of God. In Scripture, we encounter the living Word. In that sense, it becomes the word of God to us. However, Scripture cannot be described as the Word of God in and of itself.

The argument contains important truths but presented like this it misconstrues biblical emphases, imperils the doctrine of inspiration and damages the gospel message. The distinction between Christ, the living Word, and Scripture, the written Word, must certainly be recognized. The Bible itself makes this distinction. Christ is depicted as the incarnate Word through whom God finally addressed mankind. The word of the gospel, sometimes simply called 'the word', is seen as the means of communicating the good news about Christ. The Bible, however, assures us that Christ, the living Word, addresses us through Scripture, the written Word.

The inspiration of Scripture is a truth which ought to be cherished by all Christians. Equally dear are the truths that the gospel produces a hearing which leads to faith and that regeneration by the Spirit comes regularly through the word of Scripture. We must, of course, admit in the latter case that this is not an absolute necessity. To claim that it was would be to limit the Spirit of God. The Bible, however, frequently presents the Word as the instrument of regeneration and faith. Jesus claimed that it was through the words given to him by God and spoken to his followers that they came to believe in him as Messiah (John 17:8). He commands that his words remain in his followers as the means of their spiritual growth (John 15:7-8). Paul reminds Christians at Rome that faith comes through hearing and hearing through the word of Christ (Rom. 10:17). He assures his young friend Timothy that Scripture gives knowledge of salvation through faith in Jesus the Messiah (2 Tim. 3:15). James sees regeneration as God choosing to give a person birth through the word of truth, a kind of new species issuing from God's mouth (James 1:18). Peter, as we have seen, traces new birth back to the imperishable seed of God's Word (1 Peter 1:23-25).

Rather than seeing a false dichotomy between Christ and Scripture, our view of the Bible ought to be Christ-centred. The entire Old Testament is the prophetic word about Christ the living Word. The Gospels are the fulfilment of this as they relate the life and teaching of Jesus the Messiah. Acts discloses the historical outworking of the Christ who has come. The New Testament letters explore the implications of Christ and his teaching. Revelation anticipates the return of the living Word as King and Judge of all men. Our present study of Christ in Isaiah is a particular application of this general theme that the New is in the Old concealed; the Old is in the New revealed. Through this approach, we hear the living Word address us through the written Word by the power of the Spirit of God. The Christ of Isaiah brings salvation to his people for he acts as Prophet, Priest and King.

4.
The work of Christ

Isaiah 42 brings us a new and radical view of the coming Messiah. He is described as God's Servant: 'Here is my servant, whom I uphold, my chosen one in whom I delight' (Isa. 42:1).

This is radically new in Isaiah, a theme which the prophet goes on to develop. He has just spoken of the nation as God's servant in similar language:

'But you, O Israel, my servant,
Jacob, whom I have chosen,
you descendants of Abraham my friend,
I took you from the ends of the earth,
from its farthest corners I called you.
I said, "You are my servant";
I have chosen you and have not rejected you'

(Isa. 41:8-9).

Now it is different. The figure of the Servant is much more personal. The details are more easily referred to an individual than to a nation. This is also the case as Isaiah continues to develop this theme of 'the Servant of the Lord' (Isa. 49:1-6; 50:4-9; 52:13 - 53:12). Hundreds of years later the Ethiopian treasurer had a problem as he read from the prophet Isaiah in his chariot. 'Tell me, please, who is the prophet talking about, himself or someone else?' he asked Philip (Acts 8:34). He obviously had detected the difference. Philip referred the fulfilment of this prophecy to Jesus.

Servant

For Isaiah to describe the coming deliverer as a 'servant' would in some sense have been strange. It was one thing to categorize God's people in bondage in this way, but quite another to view their deliverer in these terms. The servant played a submissive role. He had limited personal rights and was bound to obey his master. Often his tasks were menial and his position in society usually inferior. Viewed in this light, the idea of the champion of God's people as a servant would be intolerable.

On the other hand, servants in Hebrew society were not the nonentities that such a position implied among other peoples. Obedience was the mark of the servant, but this did not necessarily include servility. Officers of the king were called servants and in no way might this be regarded as a 'degraded' status. Eliezer held this position in Abraham's household, as did Joseph in Egypt. Those who distinguished themselves in service for God were described as his servants, for example, Abraham (Gen. 26:24), Moses (Exod. 14:31) and David (2 Sam. 3:18). The title 'servant of the Lord' had both a humble and exalted side to it.

For all that, any idea of servanthood connected with the coming Messiah would have been novel. Anything Isaiah had previously said on the subject had certainly not included that element. There was the idea of the Messiah exercising government as a king, a descendant of the house of David. There was even the prophecy about the birth of such a ruler. But Isaiah's oracles, like the thoughts of the psalmist, centred on a dominant figure, a ruler continuing the line of the throne of Judah, not a servant. In Jewish thought, there was nothing menial or servile about Israel's deliverer. The Messiah would be a second Adam ushering in an era of peace and prosperity, a prophet virile in leadership like Moses, a son of David ruling over God's people with justice, a branch from the same dynasty bringing back the glory of that kingdom, a son of man interceding with God on behalf of his people, but never a servant. Servility was unworthy of such a dignified office.

Yet this is the precise aspect which Isaiah stresses as he previews the 'Servant of the Lord'. His humiliation, his obedience and his suffering are all underlined. The Servant works quietly and tenderly, not loudly and harshly (Isa. 42:2-4). He faces opposition with patience and pursues God's purpose with determined obedience (Isa. 50:5-9). He is disfigured beyond recognition and suffers sacrificially for God's people (Isa. 52:13 - 53:12). The Servant's suffering is his glory; his obedience is his strength. Even though that obedience is primarily directed towards Jehovah, whose servant he is, his involvement in degradation and servility is obvious. These were entirely new emphases in the forecast of a coming deliverer. Such a concept was bound to sound strange in the ears of the hearers as Israel languished in Babylonian captivity. To many it would represent a forlorn dream rather than a triumphant hope. When Isaiah went so far as to describe

Cyrus the pagan king as God's 'anointed', his words must have seemed incredible (Isa. 45:1). But this was the word of the Lord. This was the message of God's prophet. The Messiah would be a Suffering Servant.

The transformation which Isaiah's servant Messiah brought to the Old Testament expectation of a coming deliverer was colossal. The fulfilment of this aspect of prophecy in the New Testament is remarkable. Traditional anticipation of a conquering Messianic King is pushed aside as the gospel insists on a Suffering Servant.

The ministry of Jesus

This theme is prominent in Jesus' ministry. Constantly he avoided being acclaimed as Christ and he frequently dissuaded those who did so acknowledge him from publicizing it further. Immediately after Peter confessed Jesus as Christ, he enjoined silence on that matter and began to teach how the Son of Man had to suffer many things from the religious leaders, be put to death and rise again. Jesus continued this teaching shortly afterwards at his transfiguration and later when the disciples squabbled among themselves about leadership. On this latter occasion, he reminded his disciples, in words strongly echoing Isaiah, that the Son of Man came not to be served, but to serve, and to give his life as a ransom for many (Mark 10:45).

Jesus was educating his followers on the subject of a servant Messiah. When, before his death, he tied a towel around his waist and washed his disciples' feet, he was acting out before them the precise meaning of this important lesson. Aware that he had come from God, Jesus got up from his chair, leaving the throne of his authority. He took off his outer garments, laying aside his eternal glory. He assumed servanthood in the towel, water and basin, in washing and drying his disciples' feet. He anticipated ascension and glorification in putting on his clothes and in returning to his place. The lesson is pointed and meaningful, perhaps the clearest example in the New Testament of Christ's servanthood.

The significance of Isaiah's Servant in Jesus' own thinking and teaching is staggering. Jesus chose the title Son of Man, his own favourite Old Testament description of himself, and used it to convey much of what was predicted of Isaiah's Servant. The Son of Man must suffer, comes not to be served, but to serve, seeks and saves the lost. In this way the regal dignity of the Son of Man is linked with the lowly condescension of Isaiah's Servant. Exaltation and humility blend in perfect harmony in Jesus as they did in Isaiah's Servant of the Lord. This also, in large measure, accounts for Jesus' reluctance to accept publicly the designation 'Christ', since in popular opinion Christ would come to lord it over his enemies, expel the hated Romans and make Israel a great nation — a kingdom quite obviously of this world. While Jesus never used the term 'servant' to describe himself as Messiah, the prominence of obedience and suffering in his life and teaching gives the impression that at times the word trembled on his lips. Certainly, the importance of Isaiah's Servant is written large on the Gospel records of Jesus' ministry.

Any view of Jesus' work which discounts this is defective and inconsistent with how Jesus himself saw his mission on earth. He came not primarily as healer, teacher, miracle-worker, or even as ruler. He came to obey, to suffer and to die. Those other aspects of his work find purpose and meaning only in this. His kingdom, which was not of this world, was established strangely through his death. His lordship arises not from his defeat by wicked men, but from his vindication by God. The gospel he embodies and the work he accomplishes are of the same nature. Through suffering and dying Christ heals, teaches, transforms and rules. Christ is above all the Saviour of his people. Through this process Isaiah's Servant moulds his mission.

The understanding of the church

This 'servant' theme is also the key to the early church's understanding of who Jesus was. Peter attributed the power by which the crippled man was healed to God's holy servant Jesus. The church in prayer rejoiced in the victory of the same Servant as Peter and John were freed from the Jewish council. Philip evangelized the Ethiopian treasurer by pointing him to the fulfilment of Isaiah's Servant in Jesus of Nazareth. Today's church, with its increasingly diminishing role in secular society, must return to the same allegiance. She must proclaim the power, praise the victory and preach the gospel of the Servant of the Lord, Jesus of Nazareth. She must do this with unremitting boldness and with unapologetic authority. Her understanding of the person of her Lord must reflect, above all, his suffering servanthood. That understanding must permeate her gospel preaching. She must proclaim the obedience of his life and the suffering of his death, both as a priority and as a prophetic fulfilment of the Old Testament, if she is to see her Lord glorified.

The servant theme also permeates the apostolic witness. For Paul, Jesus' servanthood is the pattern of true humility. He who was in the form of God took on himself the form of a servant. He emptied himself and became obedient to death on the cross. As his followers, Christians have no option but to do the same. The demon of pride and false humility can only be exorcised from the church when she moves in that direction. After the example of Christ, the servant mind empties of self and produces true humility. Only then will the church be like her Lord. What a curse pride is among Christians today, in its subtler forms of intellectual superiority, materialistic acquisition and self-esteem, as compared with the social snobbery of a past generation! Only Christ-mindedness can rid her of this scourge. Her members must have within them the mind of this Servant.

For Peter, Jesus' condescension is an example of patience. As Jesus suffered in silence before Pilate and his accusers, so Christian slaves scattered throughout Asia Minor must bear the tyranny of harsh masters with fortitude and obedience (1 Peter 2:18-25). The remarkable thing was that the immediate consequence of the Servant's gospel was not the abolition of slavery (though that was an ultimate and necessary implication), but the obedience of slaves, even when wrongly treated. Christian patience today in a 'liberated' society must be of the same quality. Paul sees this behaviour as a means of making doctrine attractive: 'Teach slaves to be subject to their masters in everything, to try to please them, not to talk back to them, and not to steal from them, but to show that they can be fully trusted, so that in every way they will make the teaching about God our Saviour attractive' (Titus 2:9-10).

For the writer to the Hebrews, Jesus' humility is an integral part of his sympathetic priesthood. Jesus cried and prayed to God and was heard because he was submissive. Although he was a Son, yet he learned obedience through his suffering. In this way the great High Priest becomes the source of eternal salvation for all who obey him. Again, Christ's suffering is to the fore: a suffering which not only assures of sympathy, but saves from sin. The exalted and humble aspects of Isaiah's Servant are both fulfilled in Christ's priesthood, divine in his saving power and human in his obedient suffering. This is the Servant of Isaiah, the Jesus of Nazareth who is proclaimed in the gospel.

In this striking way, the new and strange 'servant' work of Isaiah's Messiah becomes the leading motif in Jesus' ministry, the church's message and the apostolic teaching. The idea of a servant Messiah gains the day. All other prophecies give way to this theme. They find fulfilment in it.

Healer

Isaiah introduces the work of Christ the Servant by portraying him as a healer:

'Here is my servant, whom I uphold,
   my chosen one in whom I delight;
I will put my Spirit on him
   and he will bring justice to the nations.
He will not shout or cry out,
   or raise his voice in the streets.
A bruised reed he will not break,
   and a smouldering wick he will not snuff out.
In faithfulness he will bring forth justice;
   he will not falter or be discouraged
till he establishes justice on earth.
   In his law the islands will put their hope'

(Isa. 42:1-4).

The Servant carries out this healing work under the Spirit's anointing. God has chosen him, takes a delight in him and puts his Spirit on him. Isaiah had earlier predicted how the Spirit of the Lord would rest on the Messiah, aiding him in his government as King (Isa. 11:1-5). There the emphasis was on the permanence and effectiveness of the Spirit's anointing, a lordly, judicial activity. Here the stress is on the love and delight from which the anointing arises and the sensitive way in which the Servant carries out his task. The task is essentially the same — that of government, bringing justice to the nations. The emphasis here, however, is on the meekness and quietness by which the servant Messiah works. His approach is more that of a healer than a ruler.

The early days of Jesus' ministry follow this precise pattern. As we have already seen, it is Luke who describes Jesus' baptism as the occasion of his anointing by the Spirit for his life's work. The voice from heaven at Jesus' baptism, mentioned by the Gospel writers, affirms that Jesus is God's Son, whom God loves and with whom he is well pleased (Matt. 3:17; Mark 1:11; Luke 3:22). The same voice of authority assures the frightened disciples of Jesus' true identity at the transfiguration (Matt. 17:5; Mark 9:7; Luke 9:35). The sentiments expressed by the voice are precisely those of Isaiah: here is the Messiah chosen by God in whom God takes great delight. The anointing of the servant Messiah is fulfilled in the baptism of Jesus. The authority of the Spirit accompanies the display of the Servant's glory at his transfiguration.

When Jesus begins his ministry, he continues the theme of repentance proclaimed by John the Baptist. But he is also deeply involved in a work of healing. All varieties of sick folk are brought to him for healing, including even the demon-possessed and lepers, and in tender compassion Jesus heals them. Mark, at the outset of his Gospel record, stresses that Jesus was aware of the priority of his saving work. All were seeking his healing, but Jesus would press on to other villages to preach there also (Mark 1:38). That was his primary task. Jesus displays the same love and care in healing of the souls of men and women as he does in healing their bodies. A tender healing of the soul is the servant Messiah's method of establishing the rule of his kingdom, just as Isaiah's Servant would bring justice to the nations in a humble and quiet manner.

Sympathy

Isaiah forecasts this in precise detail. It is the tenderness of the Servant's work which strikes us immediately.

> 'He will not shout or cry out,
>   or raise his voice in the streets.
> A bruised reed he will not break…'

(Isa. 42:2-3).

The Servant goes quietly about his business. No brash statements come from his lips. No raucous sentiments mark his approach. He deals gently with the bruised of mankind. What a vivid picture the 'bruised reed' presents! The solitary reed, clipped by the wing of a bird, hangs lifeless among the other rushes, its life-giving sap restricted, its resistance to the driving wind nil. How easily it could be snapped off and for ever forgotten and lost! The Servant restores it, lifts it up, replenishes its growth, heals its defects and makes it live again.

How applicable this is to the ministry of Jesus! He hears the commotion and sees the crowd. They thrust the woman before him and cite the law to him, condemning her because she has been taken in the very act of adultery. Jesus writes on the ground as though ignoring them and calls for the sinless to cast the first stone. They all slink away until she stands alone before him. He asks for her accusers. There are none. Neither will he accuse her, but she must leave her sin. The Servant condemns her sin, but forgives the sinner. How good to know the Servant still plies his gentle role, lifting up the bruised and broken, healing the soul-sick, restoring the fallen! He does not barge into lives without invitation, but with quiet care attracts the lone and lost to himself. Yet he is merciless towards sin, as forthright in condemning it as he is in forgiving the sinner. Christians have much to learn in personal evangelism from studying the Servant's method. Too often they are loud and unfeeling when they should be quiet and loving.

Patience

Patience is another mark of the Servant's work:

> '... and a smouldering wick he will not snuff out.
> In faithfulness he will bring forth justice;
>   he will not falter or be discouraged
> till he establishes justice on earth.
>   In his law the islands will put their hope'
>
>   (Isa. 42:3-4).

The wicks of oil-lamps needed constant trimming. A past generation knew this in a way unknown today. The flickering flame was to them the sure sign of what was needed. The glass was removed and the crusted black soot scraped from the wick. This meant that the flame would burn brightly again. Care was necessary, for in this process the flame could easily be snuffed out. Think also of the patience needed in lighting a fire in the old days and cajoling the flame into life by placing a newspaper over the front of the fire. The frustration was often great and repeated efforts were needed. It usually required much patience before one eventually saw a roaring fire in the grate.

The Servant works patiently at his task. There is a dogged commitment marking his activity, which is not the result of frustrated anger, but of quiet confidence. He has his aim in view. It impels him forward, dispels discouragement and quickens his work. Eventually he establishes his rule, a rule of justice and hope.

Peter's experience recalls this patient treatment. Jesus dealt with Peter in this way at every point. When he sank in the waves, Jesus firmly rescued him. When he rebelled against the approaching sufferings of the Son of Man, Jesus sternly rebuked him. When he boasted of his allegiance, Jesus warned him. When Satan would have sifted him like wheat, Jesus prayed for him. When his denial drove him to despair, Jesus recalled and restored him. What a problem Peter posed! For all this, the servant Messiah never faltered. With fitting instruction and persistent care he established his rule in the life of this unsteady man. He must do the same with us today. He is the Servant who sets his face like a flint to go to Jerusalem. Having loved his followers, he loved them right to the end. Peter learned that lesson in a way he would never forget.

How comforting to see tenderness combined with patience! Tenderness alone might fail. However sensitive, it reaches the point of frustration and then gives up. But linked to patience, it gains a persistence which leads to success. What a great comfort it is to realize that the Servant treats people like this! He identifies with our situation, sympathizes with our plight and continues until his purpose is accomplished. He is the God who heals backslidings and loves freely. More even than this, he actually restores the years the locusts have eaten. God is expert in healing. Christians need to follow Christ's example in this. They must not be harsh, but tender with one another. They must cultivate patience in all relationships. People and their attitudes are the primary problem of the church. Often it is not opposition outside but friction within that most threatens Christ's body. The apostles constantly point to the servant Messiah in order that these lessons might be learned: Paul to Christ's humility of mind, Peter to his patient suffering and John to his selfless love.

The importance of Isaiah's prophecy

Now the combination of tenderness and patience in Jesus' ministry need not necessarily derive from Isaiah's Servant. The quietness and sympathy of Christ's approach may have a more general background. Is there any reason to tie these traits particularly to Isaiah's prophecy, to see this as the express motivation behind Jesus' thoughts and actions?

Two things point forcefully in that direction. First, there are, as we have already noted, those times when Jesus as Son of Man quite self-consciously fulfils Servant prophecies. Secondly, there is the explicit witness of Matthew.

Matthew attributes Jesus' withdrawal from controversy with the religious leaders and his silence on the subject of being the Messiah to this Servant prophecy. Matthew notes how a Sabbath healing by Jesus led to a plot by the Pharisees to kill him. The story continues: 'Aware of this, Jesus withdrew from that place. Many followed him, and he healed all their sick, warning them not to tell who he was. This was to fulfil what was spoken through the prophet Isaiah:

"Here is my servant whom I have chosen,
    the one I love, in whom I delight;
I will put my Spirit on him,
    and he will proclaim justice to the nations.
He will not quarrel or cry out;
    no one will hear his voice in the streets.
A bruised reed he will not break,
    and a smouldering wick he will not snuff out,
till he leads justice to victory.
    In his name the nations will put their hope"'

(Matt. 12:15-21).

This is a remarkable statement, particularly in the light of the many occasions when Jesus engaged the religious leaders in debate and triumphed over them. He did not fear controversy. On some occasions he actually invited it by taking the battle to his enemies. Here, however, he withdraws from controversy, enjoins silence and continues quietly a ministry of healing. Matthew explains Jesus' behaviour as a fulfilment of Isaiah's prophecy.

Looking at the subject of the Servant's identity from another vantage-point, Homer Hailey reaches a similar conclusion: 'The servant has been variously identified. Cyrus has been suggested, as have been the prophets (collective) of God. Whybray holds that Deutero-Isaiah, whom he assumes to have been the writer of chapters 40-46, is in view, whereas Willis suggests Israel the nation. The vast majority of conservative commentators support the view that the servant is the Messiah, the Lord Jesus of the New Testament. When the servant's mission is considered (vv. 1-9), it becomes clear that only Christ fulfils the assignment; all others fall short. He alone is the instrument of Israel's restoration and redemption, a light to the Gentiles, and the establisher of justice on the earth. Also, the means he used in accomplishing his mission sets him apart from any of the other suggestions. Matthew settles the question when he quotes the opening verses of Isaiah 42 and applies them to Jesus (Matt. 12:15-21).'

Christ not only fulfils the prophecy of Isaiah's Servant; he consciously directs the details of his ministry by means of it. Jesus intentionally views himself as Isaiah's Servant. This point calls for reflection. There can be no doubt that Jesus saw himself as fulfilling many of the great Old Testament predictions of the Messiah. He regarded himself as great David's greater Son, as Daniel's majestic Son of Man, as greater than Abraham, Moses, Jonah and Solomon. But that which shapes most his self-consciousness as Messiah was Isaiah's Servant. The quiet side of Jesus' work; his withdrawal from public acclaim and, at times, from dispute; his enforced silence on the subject of his messiahship; his informal instruction of the Twelve, like a rabbi with his followers; his humility, tenderness and patience in personal encounter — all these drew inspiration from the servant Messiah and form a prelude to Christ's suffering on Calvary.

The response of the church

This aspect of Christ's work also calls for response. The servant Messiah begets a servant church. If Jesus, their Lord and Teacher, had washed his disciples' feet, then they also as his servants should wash one another's feet. This must be so on the individual level. The humility, tenderness and patience which Christ displayed must be reflected in the lives of his followers. This will at times mean withdrawing from the controversy, not out of fear and cowardice, but out of wisdom. Divisive quarrelling can overshadow rather than clarify essentials. Arid controversy hardens rather than helps relationships. A soul is sometimes best won by avoiding an argument. Christians must lead quiet and peaceable lives and they must not be quarrelsome. It is important to learn the lesson of agreeing to disagree. This does not mean compromising the truth or failing to defend it. It simply means representing it in the best way possible.

Corporately, the church needs to move in this direction also. Serving the Lord Christ means learning to serve one another. Faction and party strife rupture fellowship. Schism is a sin which rends the body of Christ. In this, the cause of truth must never suffer. A servant church must not be confused, but biblical in its doctrine. The secret lies not just in speaking the truth, but in speaking the truth in love (Eph. 4:15). A servant church does not mean a defenceless church, where the gospel is secondary. Where would the church have been without the great Christian apologists of an earlier day — the Justin Martyrs of a past era who defended the church against charges of cannibalism and infanticide and advanced a theology of the human and divine Word against a world in the grip of Graeco-Roman philosophy? The church has had its apologists in the past and needs them today, recalling God's people to scriptural truth, defining faith according to biblical norms, defending the gospel in an increasingly secular society. Yet even in this the church is to be a servant church, choosing wisely the battles in which to engage and recognizing when it is better to desist. There is a time for controversy and a time to refrain from controversy.

Redeemer

The Servant who heals also redeems. The King stoops to conquer. The quiet side of the Messiah's work — restoring, caring, renewing — is matched by a public activity, that of liberating, subduing and ruling. The Servant does the one almost imperceptibly, with great tenderness and patience. He does the other quite openly, with great majesty and power. This is perfectly consistent with the function of a servant in Hebrew society. While obedience and service were expected, dignity and efficiency were also anticipated. This was especially so in the case of servants of the king. It would naturally be required of the Servant of the Lord.

The creative power of God

The Servant, who heals under the anointing of the Spirit, also redeems under the appointment of God the Creator.

'This is what God the Lord says—
he who created the heavens and stretched them out,
    who spread out the earth and all that comes out of it,
who gives breath to its people,
    and life to those who walk on it:
"I, the Lord, have called you in righteousness;
    I will take hold of your hand"'

(Isa. 42:5-6).

Creation is seen as a majestic act of God throughout the Old Testament. Moses gives us that panoramic view at the very outset. God calls all things into existence from nothing in six days by the sheer power of his word. All creation — sky, earth, sea, sun, moon, stars, vegetation, fish, animals, mankind — have their source of being in a life-giving God. David sees man as the crown of this creation. Man is God's vicegerent on earth to control and subdue creation. Yet how small is man amid all of this! What honour God bestows on man in granting him such a position, made in God's likeness, after God's image!

Isaiah gasps too at the majesty of God as Creator. Man is as nothing before him. The nations are a mere drop in the bucket; the teeming millions are like grasshoppers before him. Here Isaiah once again praises God as Creator, but in this instance to maximize the importance of his Servant, rather than to stress the insignificance of man within his creation. Calvin writes, 'On this account he brings forward clear proofs of the power of God, that all may be aroused by the mention of them, and may be convinced that he who created all things out of nothing, who spread out the heavens, who produced vegetation, who gave life to animals and who upholds and defends all things by his power, will easily perform what he promises concerning the reign of Christ.' God the Creator calls, empowers and sustains the servant Messiah.

The New Testament ripples with this fulfilment. It is not simply that Jesus as Son sustains a unique relationship with God his Father. The very creative power of God undergirds all Jesus' acts. His Father God works, so he works. All power is given to him in heaven and on earth. Jesus breathes the Spirit on his disciples, empowering them to remit or to retain sins. By the authority of God, Jesus exorcises demons. The eternal Word, through whom everything was made, becomes flesh in the person of Jesus of Nazareth. The eternal Son, who upholds all things by the word of his power, is God's final word to mankind. God who said, 'Let light shine out of darkness,' has shone in our hearts to give the light of the knowledge of the glory of God in the face of Christ. The creative power of God is at all points evident in the life of Jesus. There is invariably a link between God's creation through the eternal Son, and God's new creation through the God-man Jesus. The Servant has upon him the divine imprimatur of creative authority. He who is the agent of creation is the source of regeneration.

Christ's work is powerful, for behind it lies all the authority of God. Christ's work shatters the stranglehold of sin over man and frees him from its grasp.

> He breaks the power of cancelled sin
> He sets the prisoner free.
>
> (Charles Wesley)

Old habits are broken, harmful associations severed, a new life comes into being. We ought to look unashamedly for evidence of this. Today vague commitment has too often replaced vital conversion. There is a destructive side to the work of Christ. Satan is bound and sin's rule ends. This makes a vast difference, even for the most upright person. Christ's work is also creative. It breathes life into dead souls. New desires and interests arise. Prayer and the Bible become priorities. Fellowship with other Christians becomes a natural longing. The expulsive power of a new affection, as Thomas Chalmers described it, redirects living. Character is moulded and transformed. Friendships are changed in this process. If anyone is in Christ, there is a new creation — the old has gone, the new has come. Christians are God's workmanship, created in Christ for good deeds. Sadly, too little is known of this decisive, transforming power and its practical results today. It is, none the less, the nature of the work of Christ. It testifies to the power of Christ's saving gospel.

A covenant for the people

Isaiah specifies the Servant's redeeming work as based on a covenant: 'I will keep you and will make you to be a covenant for the people' (Isa. 42:6).

The idea of deliverance through a covenant would not have been unusual for Israel. From the earliest days that was how God had revealed himself to Israel. They were essentially his people. They belonged to him and, in the most reverential of ways, he belonged to them. They were his people; he was their God. The entire ethos of their religion rested on the foundation that they were God's covenant people. God had bound them to himself by solemn oath or covenant. The unfolding saga of their national history made this clear. God had established his covenant with their founder Abraham, renewed it with Moses in their deliverance from Egypt and confirmed it to David and his dynasty for ever.

The personal note

What was new here, however, was the way in which this great relationship was expressed. The covenant was personalized in the servant Messiah. God would make him to be a covenant for the people. The covenant was no longer to be thought of merely as a contract or treaty, with binding stipulations, promising God's protection while requiring his people's obedience. The covenant was supremely a person, one through whom God would ratify and realize all the blessings he had promised, one to whom they would be bound by the response of obedience. A personal mediator replaces a paper contract. The Servant epitomizes all of God's covenant intentions towards his people. F. Delitzsch sees this as further proof that the Servant is neither Israel nor Isaiah, but the Messiah, 'the personal bond which unites Israel and its God in a new fellowship'.

To some extent this had already been anticipated in the Old Testament. The seed of the woman would destroy the seed of the serpent. In Abraham's seed all families of the earth would be blessed. The ruler of the eternal kingdom would be a successor of David's dynasty. But never had the full implications been so openly stated as here by Isaiah. Even Jeremiah's prediction of a new covenant, with all its exciting promises, was not couched in these personal terms. Isaiah reaches the high-water mark of Old Testament prophecy in a personal covenant Messiah.

The same personal note pervades the New Testament fulfilment. Jesus was born because God swore in covenant oath to Abraham, Isaac and Jacob. Jesus died claiming his blood to be that of the new covenant. Jesus rose from death through the blood of the eternal covenant. Christ is the seed to whom the covenant promises were made. All the promises of God reach fulfilment in him. He is the mediator of a new and better covenant.

The warmth of a personal relationship

This means that Christians get the best of both worlds. As Abraham's children, they inherit all the blessings of the covenant. That radical newness of which Jeremiah spoke is theirs. God places his law in their hearts, causes them to know him, from the least of them to the greatest, makes them his people and forgives all their sins. But they receive all this through a warm, personal relationship with Christ. Through Christ, the blessing of Abraham comes to the Gentiles. Through him, they receive the promised Spirit by faith. All the rich blessings of a covenant relationship with God flow to Christians through their Saviour Jesus. There is nothing formal or cold about their faith. It is not merely a contract drawn up to which they give assent and receive in return God's forgiveness and protection. It is rather a firm and sure relationship with God which they enjoy through Jesus the mediator, who is with them day by day through the Spirit.

Lidie H. Edmunds expresses this warmth in her hymn:

My faith has found a resting-place,
Not in device nor creed
I trust the ever-living One,
His wounds for me shall plead.

This is not decrying the importance of setting out clearly the great covenant blessings we inherit through Christ. It is simply reminding us that we receive all these through the person of Jesus our mediator. The *Westminster Confession* stipulates those blessings in rich language: 'It pleased God, in his eternal purpose, to choose and ordain the Lord Jesus his only begotten Son, to be the Mediator between God and man; the Prophet, Priest and King; the Head and Saviour of his Church; the Heir of all things; and Judge of the world; unto whom he did from all eternity give a people to be his seed, and to be by him in time redeemed, called, justified, sanctified and glorified' (*Westminster Confession,* 8:1). Isaiah's Servant is the covenant mediator of God's people.

Light for the Gentiles

Isaiah's Servant is also a light for the Gentile world. The Redeemer of God's people extends his power beyond the limits of Israel to the nations:

'I will keep you and will make you
    to be a covenant for the people
    and a light for the Gentiles,
to open eyes that are blind,

to free captives from prison
and to release from the dungeon those who sit in darkness.

'I am the Lord; that is my name!
   I will not give my glory to another
   or my praise to idols.
See, the former things have taken place,
   and new things I declare;
before they spring into being
   I announce them to you'

(Isa. 42:6-9).

This was decidedly new. Israel had always been conscious of being God's chosen people, a race apart. Had God not promised they would triumph over all their enemies? Had God not given to them exclusively the law to teach them, the prophets to guide them and the temple to symbolize his presence among them? In their darkest days Israel held firmly to these things. Whatever the situation, God would protect and care for them. He would defeat their enemies. He would restore their land. They were expressly forbidden to mingle in marriage with the Gentile nations. The thought of their coming Messiah being a light to the Gentiles would not only be offensive, but intolerable for them. It was at variance with their faith in the God of Abraham, Isaac and Jacob.

The story of Jonah illustrates this so well. Jonah fled from God not just because Nineveh was a notoriously wicked place, nor even because it was so large that the thought of preaching against it was virtually impossible. Jonah fled from God because Nineveh was a Gentile city, enemy territory, the Assyrian capital. If Jonah went to Nineveh he would have been branded a false prophet, a traitor to God's covenant people Israel. God had to pursue Jonah across the sea, to send a storm and to prepare a fish to change Jonah's attitude. Even after the repentance of Nineveh, God had to persuade his angry and disgruntled servant of the divine purpose to care in love for this Gentile city with all its inhabitants, child and beast: 'But Nineveh has more than a hundred and twenty thousand people who cannot tell their right hand from their left, and many cattle as well. Should I not be concerned about that great city?' (Jonah 4:11).

The purpose of God

Israel had to be taught that the God of Abraham cared about the Gentile nations and in this Isaiah was their teacher. There had been hints in this direction from the earliest days. The promise to Abraham had been that all people on earth would be blessed through him. Not infrequently Gentiles prospered through Israelite individuals, as Potiphar did through Joseph. David even forecasts that the nations will come to the Messiah and will be blessed through him. But the practicalities of this were never really thought through and it remained largely the pipedream of a future Messianic age, an age of Israelite supremacy and Gentile inferiority.

Isaiah explains the details quite differently. He had already prophesied a Messiah who would judge among the nations. He had even foretold a time when God's blessing would be shared by Israel's enemies: 'The Lord Almighty will bless them, saying, "Blessed be Egypt my people, Assyria my handiwork, and Israel my inheritance"' (Isa. 19:25). Here he affirms that the Servant who is a covenant for God's people will also be a light for the Gentiles. The Servant will accomplish this by enlightening the blind and releasing the prisoners. These are among the 'new things' God is declaring. They will be fulfilled just as surely as the 'former things' have taken place. The child Messiah to be born will not only enlighten Zebulun and Naphtali, but Galilee among the Gentiles (Isa. 9:1). The servant Messiah who comes fulfils a dual role of being a covenant for Israel and a light for the Gentiles. The nations will eventually be included in the people of God. God will bring about a new Israel through his servant Messiah, a new Israel comprising both Jews and Gentiles. Isaiah is not merely foretelling the restoration of Israel from Babylonian captivity through Cyrus, God's anointed; he is proclaiming the conversion of the Gentiles to the coming Christ.

Indeed, in this whole process Israel has a significant part to play. Isaiah begins here to unfold the theme that God's choice of Israel is towards that very end and that through Israel's seed, the servant Messiah, the Gentiles will be drawn into the people of God. God's election has in view the salvation of the Gentiles. The covenant and the light to the Gentiles are inextricably bound together.

The pattern of this purpose is obvious in the New Testament fulfilment of Isaiah's prophecy. Jesus reveals himself as Messiah to the Samaritan woman at Sychar in spite of his disciples' disaffection. Jesus finds in a Roman centurion greater faith than in all Israel. He succumbs to the plea of a Greek woman to exorcise her daughter. Though conscious of being sent first and foremost to the lost sheep of Israel, Jesus is yet clearly aware that there are other sheep not of that fold whom he must reach. His closing words to his followers prescribe that very situation. They would be witnesses to him in Jerusalem, Judea, Samaria and throughout the world. The unfolding sequence of the Spirit's outpouring confirms this promise — on the Jews at Pentecost, the Samaritans through Philip, the Gentiles in Cornelius' home. It is significant that the disciples were first called 'Christ's ones' where the light broke into the Gentile darkness at Antioch. Paul repeatedly, having preached to Jews, turns from them to evangelize Gentiles. He explains this as part of God's saving purpose: branches are broken off the natural olive-tree, Israel, so that the Gentiles might be grafted in. The blessing of Abraham comes on the Gentiles through Jesus the Messiah. The Servant is both covenant to Israel and light to Gentiles.

This inspires confidence as the church seeks to evangelize the world. The purpose of God underlies the command of Jesus in the Great Commission: 'All authority in heaven and on earth has been given to me. Therefore go and make disciples of all nations, baptizing them in the name of the Father and of the Son and of the Holy Spirit, and teaching them to obey everything I have commanded you. And surely I will be with you, to the very end of the age' (Matt. 28:18-20). As Christians go out to win an alien world for Christ, they go in the knowledge that this is God's purpose in his Messiah and that God's purpose will invariably be fulfilled. Whatever disrupts their progress, hinders their efforts or depresses their spirits, they must return to this purpose and renew their flagging zeal through it. The promise of Isaiah, the commission of Jesus, the progress of the early church and the teaching of the apostles are the banners under which they march and which inspire them in this.

The power of God

Not only the purpose, but the power of God underlies the command of Jesus in the Great Commission. As the servant Messiah went to his work anointed by God the Spirit and appointed by God the Creator, so the Son of God commissions his church to evangelize the world with all the authority of heaven and earth given to him. Christians go to win a world in Christ's name, with all the creative authority of the Servant who redeems by establishing a covenant relationship with men and women and enlightening their darkened minds in the knowledge of Christ. We must never forget the power available in proclaiming the gospel. Christ works commissioned by God's authority. He re-creates by enlightening the mind. He restores by establishing a sure and lasting relationship with God. He redeems by delivering effectively from sin's slavery. The power of the servant Messiah ensures the success of the gospel.

The completed purpose and power of this work of Christ is well expressed in the *Larger Catechism's* description of effectual calling:

'Effectual calling is the work of God's almighty power and grace whereby (out of his free and special love to his elect, and from nothing in them moving him thereunto) he doth, in his accepted time, invite and draw them to Jesus Christ, by his word and Spirit; savingly enlightening their minds, renewing and powerfully determining their wills, so that they (although in themselves dead in sin) are hereby made willing and able freely to answer his call, and to accept and embrace the grace offered and conveyed therein' (*Larger Catechism,* 67).

The work of the Servant is both tender and compelling, patient and strong. He comes as the compassionate healer to deal with man's plight, quietly and sensitively touching the sin-sick soul, restoring man effectively to spiritual health and well-being. He comes as the mighty Redeemer of his people, opening man's eyes to see his hopeless condition, liberating him from the slavery of sin, establishing a lasting relationship with him.

After Matthew records how Jesus withdrew from public controversy with the religious leaders to continue quietly his healing ministry in fulfilment of Isaiah's prophecy, he goes on to mention a very significant episode (Matt. 12:22-28). A demon-possessed man, doubly disabled, both blind and dumb, is brought to Jesus. Jesus heals him so that he can both see and speak. The Pharisees accuse Jesus of being Beelzebub, the prince of demons, and by that power casting out the demons in the sick man. Jesus, no longer avoiding controversy, joins fiercely in battle with the leaders. He exposes their accusation to ridicule. A divided kingdom, city or family cannot stand. Is Satan so divided against himself that he, Jesus, by the power of the prince of devils, casts out devils? No, the reality is quite the opposite. If he casts out devils by the Spirit of God, then the kingdom of God has come upon them. His power of exorcism symbolizes the kingdom of God, not that of Satan. Their accusation, attributing evil to good, is a sin against the Spirit of God.

It is as though Matthew is suggesting that Jesus, who in fulfilment of Isaiah's words withdraws from dispute in order to heal, now steps into the arena of conflict and displays his power to redeem. Christ exorcises this doubly distressed man, ascribes to himself the power of God's kingdom and condemns his enemies as instruments of Satan. The Servant who quietly heals mightily redeems. The Word who became flesh is yet one with the Father in creation and redemption. The Son of Man who serves and suffers will one day come as Judge. The God-man appears in a state of humiliation and in a state of exaltation. There are these two contrasting sides to the work of Christ the Servant. Isaiah introduces us to the glory of this mystery.

From heaven you came, helpless babe,
Entered our world, your glory veiled;
Not to be served but to serve,
And give your life that we might live.

There in the garden of tears,
My heavy load he chose to bear;
His heart with sorrow was torn.
'Yet not my will but yours,' he said.

Come, see his hands and his feet,
The scars that speak of sacrifice,
Hands that flung stars into space,
To cruel nails surrendered.

So let us learn how to serve,
And in our lives enthrone him.
Each other's needs to prefer
For it is Christ we're serving.

This is our God, the Servant King,
He calls us now to follow him,
To bring our lives as a daily offering
Of worship to the Servant King.

                                          (Graham Kendrick)

5.
The death of Christ

The first Servant Song proclaims the Messiah's work (Isa. 42:1-9). The fourth announces his death (Isa. 52:13 - 53:12). Two other Servant Songs link these themes. In the second, the Servant is like a sword sharpened by God to extend the kingdom beyond Jews to Gentiles (Isa. 49:1-13). In the third, the Servant sets his face like flint against ill-treatment by his enemies (Isa. 50:4-9). Efficiency and obedience mark the Servant's path from humiliation to glory. Acceptance of frustrating toil and endurance in the face of active evil accompany the patient gentleness of his work and the silent agony of his death. Suffering and success mingle in strange harmony.

The songs move in crescendo to a climax. Like a great symphony, the themes rise and fall in variations until they reach the final dramatic chorus of the Servant's death. It is a sad symphony. This accounts for some quite marked differences between the first three songs and the last. There is a difference in content, that of the Servant's work and the Servant's death. There is a difference in emphasis, for in the fourth, the purpose of the Servant's suffering is revealed. There is also a difference in presentation. In the first three, we listen to God's words about his Servant and hear the Servant's willing response. In the fourth, we gaze on the sad spectacle of the Servant's suffering and death. To change the metaphor, it is as though sight had replaced sound, a canvas presentation rather than that of an orchestral production. The effect is equally impressive. We view the strange sight of the Servant's death as the prophet unlocks the truth behind it all. A servant Messiah had always been an unusual feature. Isaiah's fourth song explains the paradox.

J. W. L. Hoad writes, 'In the description of the Servant there is progress, an individuation, as we pass from the first to the following songs. The personification becomes a Person. (G.A. Smith). "The figure that had stood half glimpsed in the shadows, as Jehovah was introducing his witness, hardly distinguishable from Israel, steps forward into the light and builds the bridge between the realities of human failure and the apparently inaccessible heights of the Divine will." (Ellison).'

An outline sketch

Isaiah first sketches the portrait in outline, but all the main features are there:

> 'See, my servant will act wisely;
>> he will be raised and lifted up and highly exalted.
> Just as there were many who were appalled at him—
>> his appearance was so disfigured beyond that of any man
>> and his form marred beyond human likeness—
> so will he sprinkle many nations,
>> and kings will shut their mouths because of him.
> For what they were not told, they will see,
>> and what they have not heard, they will understand'
>
> (Isa. 52:13-15).

Exaltation and humiliation are plainly evident. The glory and suffering of the Servant are the merging themes of his death. He is raised, lifted up, highly exalted. He is disfigured, marred, degraded. In the portrait itself, the order is reversed. The Servant's humiliation comes first, then his exaltation. Substitution marks the Servant's death: the many who were appalled at him are replaced by the many nations he will sprinkle. In the portrait proper, the substitution is specific, the reason for it made clear. Sacrifice is of the very essence of the Servant's death. 'So will he sprinkle many nations.' Sprinkling was the common Old Testament mode of cleansing. Whether it was Moses binding Israel to their vows, David pleading with God for forgiveness, the people applying the blood of the Passover lamb, the priests administering the sacrifices, or the high priest splashing the lid of the ark of the covenant, sprinkling lay at the very heart of sacrifice and spoke of cleansing. In the portrait to follow, the figure of sacrifice is boldly intensified in the Servant's death. Salvation will be the result of the Servant's death, a deliverance based on knowledge, not ignorance, on enlightenment, not confusion. Nations will see with clarity what they have not previously been told. They will understand what they have never before heard. In

the fuller portrait this is explained in terms of justification. The outline
sketch prepares us for the portrait.

Substitution

The portrait is clearly defined. It opens with a scene of substitution. This
is introduced in a strange way as Isaiah foretells the intensity of the
Servant's suffering. The humiliation of the Messiah forms the
background against which his substitution for his people is strikingly
painted.

> 'Who has believed our message
>   and to whom has the arm of the Lord been revealed?
> He grew up before him like a tender shoot,
>   and like a root out of dry ground.
> He had no beauty or majesty to attract us to him,
>   nothing in his appearance that we should desire him.
> He was despised and rejected by men,
>   a man of sorrows, and familiar with suffering.
> Like one from whom men hide their faces
>   he was despised, and we esteemed him not'
>
> (Isa. 53:1-3).

Humiliation

The opening question of the prophet expects the answer: 'No one.'
There are few who believe the message because of the nature of the
revelation. The appearance of the Messiah is singularly unattractive.
His obscure origins are not in the least noteworthy. He is like a hapless
little plant beginning to appear in barren soil, born to blossom unseen
and waste its fragrance on the desert air. The circumstances were
certainly relevant for the future: the overpowering Babylonian army,
the loneliness of exile, Jewish harps hanging silent on the willows, a
strange people in a strange land. Those were dry days for God's people
Israel. The tender shoot would be unlikely to survive in such
surroundings.

Isaiah had already mentioned these lowly origins, but not as
forcefully as here: 'A shoot will come up from the stump of Jesse; from
his roots a Branch will bear fruit' (Isa. 11:1). Doubtless Isaiah recalled
the vision God gave to him in the temple. The ruined stump of David's
dynasty would give promise of a holy seed within it. Then the
hopefulness of the prediction was paramount. Here the depressing

spectacle of circumstances threatened the Branch's very chances of survival.

But the scene is even sadder than that. The Servant's appearance is affected. He is not simply a pathetic figure, but also a despised one. Opposition, rejection, even outright enmity, have reduced him to a lonely, wearied man whose cause is frustrated and whose whole life, as a result, is sorrowful. Shame crowds in on top of all this, for his failure is attributed to the result of divine judgement: 'Yet we considered him stricken by God, smitten by him, and afflicted' (Isa. 53:4).

How significantly this was all fulfilled in the unfolding story of Jesus' life! His birth was inconspicuous in a cattle-shed in Bethlehem during a Roman census. His early days were spent in relative obscurity in the forgotten little village of Nazareth. God's chosen people still dwelt in a political, religious and moral desert. A Roman army occupied their land. An Edomite, Herod, sat on their throne. A Sadducean aristocracy manipulated their priesthood. The people themselves followed the traditions of men rather than the Word of God. Jesus taught with initial success, but this was short-lived. When people grasped the full import of his teaching, many who had followed soon left. He wept over a recalcitrant Jerusalem, educated reluctant disciples in the necessity of his suffering, was regarded as the prince of demons by his enemies, became sorrowful to the point of death in the garden and came to a degrading end through Roman crucifixion between two common thieves. Sorrowful loneliness pervaded his entire life and death in uncommon measure. The crowd who shouted, 'Hosanna!' soon cried, 'Crucify!' Pilate stood back and allowed the fury of false Jewry to attack him. His disciples forsook him and fled. Even his Father turned from him in his hour of deepest darkness. He was indeed 'a man of sorrows, and familiar with suffering'.

The Servant as substitute for his people

Isaiah sketches in this background for a particular purpose. There is a reason for the degradation of the Servant. The Servant suffers abject humiliation as a substitute for his people.

> 'Surely he took up our infirmities
>   and carried our sorrows,
> yet we considered him stricken by God,
>   smitten by him, and afflicted.
> But he was pierced for our transgressions,
>   he was crushed for our iniquities;
> the punishment that brought us peace was upon him,

and by his wounds we are healed.
We all, like sheep, have gone astray,
 each of us has turned to his own way;
and the Lord has laid on him
 the iniquity of us all'

(Isa. 53:4-6).

The substitution is drawn in the clearest possible way. The directness of the language stresses the striking equation. He took up our infirmities. He carried our sorrows. His punishment brought us peace. His wounds provide our healing. The strength of the terms emphasizes the contrast. His wounding in its intensity was piercing. His bruising was, in effect, an emotional and spiritual crushing. His chastisement was not merely disciplinary, but retributive judgement. Above all, the specific purpose of his suffering is brought out forcefully. He is marred to deal with our transgressions, our acts of rebellion against God's law and authority. He is disfigured because of our iniquities, our perversions and violations of what is right. His punishment brings not only God's forgiveness for sins, but a continuing prosperity in our relationship with God.

Isaiah stresses this as the only satisfactory explanation for the Servant's tragic condition. He is dying as a substitute for sin. He is bearing the punishment due to his people because of their radical wrongness before God. He is freeing them from its weakening and earthly effects by being sick unto death in their place. He is becoming a curse to remedy their cursed condition.

The Reformers described Jesus' humanity in the most vivid terms. The Son of God became a child so that he might for ever sanctify childhood to us, a youth to sanctify youth, a man to sanctify manhood. This is true. But the identification goes even deeper here. The servant Messiah identifies with man not simply in his humanity, but in his sinful humanity, though he himself has done no sin. The Servant substitutes for his people precisely in respect of their sin. That is the reason for his substitution and, hence, the reason for his suffering. Isaiah teaches the great truth of substitutionary atonement.

Illustrations of substitution

Early in my ministry I used to visit a man grotesquely disfigured through burns. Only with great difficulty could I bear to look at his poor face. His skin was charred, his eyes were two slits, he had no nose recognizable as such, a lipless hole formed his mouth. I knew little of the details of the fire, save that it had been caused by petrol and that he was fortunate to escape with his life. That face lived in my mind over the years, a face disfigured beyond that of any man whom I had ever known, a face from whom men hid their faces. Yet, I often thought, had my friend been burned in trying to protect his child, how differently his child would have viewed that face! What to me was a spectacle of horror and distaste, to his child would have been an object of pride and glory. His father had taken his place and been dreadfully burned instead of him. Isaiah affirms the reason for the Servant's degradation and shame so that it might be a cause of honour and joy for his people.

Abraham learnt this truth of substitution in an unforgettable way. He had sincerely believed God's promise of a son, a land and a great blessing. Yet the years crept by and no child came and his clan still remained wandering nomads. Impatient of God's providence, he took matters into his own hands and Ishmael was born. But this displeased God. Then God gave the baby Isaac to Abraham and Sarah and the sun began to shine again. How dreadful that day must have been when God told Abraham to sacrifice his son! How all rhyme and reason must have vanished from life as God determined to take away that one good thing which had happened over the years, God's very promise to him of a future posterity! But Abraham obeyed. He fetched the wood and the knife and took Isaac with him. Abraham's faith was still strong, for he told his servants to wait till he and Isaac worshipped and then they would both return. Abraham's heart must nearly have broken when his son said, 'Father, the fire and the wood are here, but where is the lamb for the burnt offering?' (Gen. 22:7). But Abraham in faith replied, 'God himself will provide the lamb for the burnt offering, my son' (Gen. 22:8). So it was. At the last moment, God intervened and Abraham saw a ram in a thicket, caught by its horns. He took the ram and offered it as a burnt offering instead of his son. Abraham called that place 'The Lord will provide'. 'On the mountain of the Lord it will be provided' was how it was known (Gen. 22:14).

Abraham, in his tortuous journey of faith, learnt what substitution meant. Isaiah drives the truth yet deeper when he describes the Servant's suffering as a substitution for sin. The seed of the woman and the son of Abraham will eventually be a substitute for sin, a servant of the Lord suffering in his people's place because of his people's sin.

The prophecy of Isaiah recalled in the New Testament

The idea of Christ's death as a substitute occurs at two important points in the Gospels: one at the outset of his ministry, at his baptism; the other at the close, prior to his death.

When John the Baptist tried to deter Jesus from being baptized, Jesus insisted, claiming that this was the proper way of fulfilling all righteousness (Matt. 3:13-17). The sinless Son received the sinner's baptism that he might identify with sinners whom he had come to save.

After the Last Supper, as Jesus predicted Peter's denial and warned his disciples of the hardships before them, he said, 'It is written, "And he was numbered with the transgressors"; and I tell you that this must be fulfilled in me. Yes, what is written about me is reaching its fulfilment' (Luke 22:37). Jesus, with the cross looming before him, regarded identification with sinners as the tragic climax of his ministry.

Both at the start and finish of his work the theme of substitution pervaded his mind. The striking feature here, however, is Jesus' self-consciousness of such a purpose and his attributing this to Isaiah's prophecy as fulfilled in himself. The link we have noticed in other aspects between Jesus' ministry and Isaiah's predictions is here quite clearly evident in his death as a substitute. Substitution is a key to Jesus' own perception of his death.

Peter had Isaiah's prophecy much in mind as he wrote his first letter. He regarded all of the prophets as serving, not themselves, but the Christian era, in their predictions of the coming Christ. But Isaiah is primary in Peter's thought. From Isaiah, Peter encourages Christians living in changing circumstances to look to the unchanging Word of God (1 Peter 1:23-25), inspires those who have entered the Christian family to lean on Christ the cornerstone (1 Peter 2:4-8) and instructs those facing persecution to learn practical lessons from Christ's death (1 Peter 2:21-24).

Peter's approach to this last topic is in some ways strange. He focuses on the substitutionary aspect of Christ's death. On two separate occasions, first dealing specifically with submission to rulers and masters and then writing more generally about suffering for doing good, this is his theme: 'To this you were called, because Christ suffered for you, leaving you an example, that you should follow in his steps.

> "He committed no sin,
>   and no deceit was found in his mouth."

'When they hurled their insults at him, he did not retaliate; when he suffered, he made no threats. Instead, he entrusted himself to him who judges justly. He himself bore our sins in his body on the tree, so that we might die to sins and live for righteousness; by his wounds you have been healed' (1 Peter 2:21-24).

'It is better, if it is God's will, to suffer for doing good than for doing evil. For Christ died for sins once for all, the righteous for the unrighteous, to bring you to God' (1 Peter 3:17-18).

This is quite remarkable. We might have expected Peter to recall in a general way Jesus' patience under suffering, but the pointed allusion to substitution, and that from Isaiah, is arresting. Why did Peter choose this approach? He did so because the problem he was addressing was not just suffering, but suffering for doing good, Christian slaves suffering at the hands of unjust masters. So, it is not simply substitution that is in view, but substitution specifically in regard to sin, the suffering of the sinless Christ in the place of sinful man. Furthermore, this is not only an example for Christians to follow, but an integral part of Christ's atoning death. It is Christ's substitution which produces a change in the sinner and provides motivation for Christian service. The death of the righteous Christ for unrighteous man conducts man into God's saving presence. Christ bears our sins in his body on the tree so that we might die to sins and live for righteousness. Substitution is necessary for the justification and sanctification which comes from Christ's atonement. There could be no clearer pointer to the importance of substitutionary atonement than this, particularly as Peter, unlike Paul in Romans, for example, is encouraging persecuted Christians rather than arguing systematic theology.

Objections to the idea of substitution

Although the idea of substitution lies at the very heart of the sufferings and death of Christ, for some this is unacceptable. They prefer to express the truth in terms of the 'representative' nature of Christ's death. Christ is our representative, our vicar, our deputy, through whose death benefits become available to man. Many pages have been written over the discussion as to the meaning of the two Greek words commonly translated by the English preposition 'for' in this context. Is the meaning 'on behalf of' or 'in the place of'? If the former, then the sense is predominantly representative; if the latter, substitutionary.

There is without doubt a representative view of Christ's death in Scripture. The designations of Christ as covenant head, second Adam and new man make this clear. But we must go further. We can claim from the passages of Scripture which we have examined that Christ is also our substitute, that he died in our place. Other scriptures point in the same direction. Christ came not to be served, but to serve, and to give his life a ransom for many (Mark 10:45). Christ gave himself as a ransom for all men (1 Tim. 2:6). In both these cases the strongest possible substitutionary terms are used. Christ redeemed us from the curse of the law by becoming a curse for us (Gal. 3:13). The natural understanding of these expressions is substitution.

Above all, however, substitution is not simply one aspect of Christ's atonement. It is specifically through substitution that the benefits of Christ's death come to his people. His wounds provide healing. His righteousness, in the place of our unrighteousness, brings us to God. His sin-bearing means that his people die to sins and live for righteousness. Christ's substitution blesses his people with justification and motivates them to sanctification. It is not simply that Christ died and rose again and, in a symbolic way, we somehow are forgiven and made ready for heaven. Christ died and rose again in our place so that we might die to sin and live to righteousness.

James Denney in his classic work *The Death of Christ*, commenting on 1 Peter 2:24, expresses this superbly: 'Once we understand what Christ's death means — once we receive the apostolic testimony that in that death He was taking all our responsibilities upon Him — no explanation may be needed. The love which is the motive of it acts immediately upon the sinful; gratitude exerts an irresistible constraint. His responsibility means our emancipation; His death our life; His bleeding wound our healing. Whoever says "He bore our sins" says substitution; and to say substitution is to say something which involves an immeasurable obligation to Christ, and has therefore in it incalculable motive power. This is the answer to some of the objections which are commonly made to the idea of substitution on moral grounds. They fail to take account of the sinner's sense of debt to Christ for what He has done, a sense of debt which it is not too much to designate as the most intimate, intense and uniform characteristic of New Testament life. It is this which bars out all ideas of being saved from the consequences of sin, while living on in sin itself. It is so profound that the whole being of the Christian is changed by it. It is so strong that it extinguishes and creates at the one time. Under the impression of it, to use the apostle's words here, the aim of Christ's bearing of our sins is fulfilled in us — we die to the sins and live to righteousness.'

Isaiah predicts this great truth, Jesus fulfils it, Peter proclaims it. May we experience it!

Sacrifice

The Suffering Servant is a sacrifice. This is the way in which he takes our place, the manner of his substitution. This aspect of the portrait is painted with great boldness. It begins with the picture of the sacrificial lamb:

'He was oppressed and afflicted,
    yet he did not open his mouth;
he was led like a lamb to the slaughter,
    and as a sheep before her shearers is silent,
    so he did not open his mouth.
By oppression and judgement he was taken away.
    And who can speak of his descendants?
For he was cut off from the land of the living;
    for the transgression of my people he was stricken.
He was assigned a grave with the wicked,
    and with the rich in his death,
though he had done no violence,
    nor was any deceit in his mouth'

                                                              (Isa. 53:7-9).

The lamb

Of all animals sheep are the most docile. Worried by dogs, they do not
retaliate. Cattle at times resist the scurrying, barking dog, but not sheep.
Even in shearing, while jostling a little, they meekly submit. The older
method of slaughtering was accompanied in the case of other animals
by squealing or braying, as though they were aware of their
forthcoming fate. But not so with sheep. They are strangely unresistant
and silent even at slaughter. Of all animals in the Jewish court of
sacrifice, the lamb was most easily led to sacrifice.

The death of the Messiah comes clearly into view now. The
sufferings of the Servant are climaxed by death. It is a tragic and silent
death. Death removed him from arrest and judgement, but it also cut
him off from his contemporaries, like a man who dies suddenly in his
prime. A grave with the wicked and rich prematurely swallows him up.
The young, docile, sacrificial lamb is the best metaphor to describe the
Servant's demise. It combines the sharpness of tragedy with the
submission to suffering.

The innocence of the victim is portrayed: 'Though he had done no
violence, nor was any deceit in his mouth.' This is the most pathetic
aspect of all. Had there been an element of guilt, had the Servant been
in any degree blameworthy, this would have given some justification
for this tragic event. But the Servant was innocent of all wrong. Because
of this, what happens is inexplicable. The incalculable value of the
ransom is thus described in terms of the slaughter of a sacrificial lamb,
with all the ritual requirements governing the selection — first of the

flock, a male of the first year having gone through all four seasons, a pure animal without spot and blemish.

Isaiah may have had the Passover lamb in mind as he predicted the Servant's death. The details are all there: the furtive silence of the slaughtering of the lamb, the tragedy of a male of the first year taken from among the flock, the innocence of a lamb without defect, the victim a substitute for the death of the first-born. All of those features were prominent on that fateful night. The people gathered in their homes. They slaughtered the lamb at twilight. They splashed the blood on the doorposts. They roasted the victim on the fire. They ate it with bitter herbs, with bread made without yeast, for there was no time to let it rise. They ate it all and burned the residue. They ate it with their cloaks tucked under their belts, their sandals on their feet, their staffs in their hands, ready to go. It was the Lord's Passover. The innocent, slaughtered lamb took the place of the favoured first-born on whom the line of the generations rested. The angel of the Lord fell upon the uncovered homes and the Israelites escaped from Egypt through the death of a lamb, cut off from the land of the living, stricken for the transgression of God's people.

Jesus, the Lamb of God

What Moses commanded and Isaiah predicted, Jesus fulfilled in striking manner. The details again are fascinating. Jesus' silence before Caiaphas and patience before Pilate, the nocturnal jostling between the Jewish Sanhedrin and the Roman tribunal, the trumped-up trial and the hurried judgement, the flogging and the cross-bearing rushed through before the Passover, the death of a man in his prime, deserted by his friends, crucified between two thieves, buried in the tomb of Joseph of Arimathea, a man joined with the wicked and the rich in his death, an innocent man in whom was no sin, who did no sin, who knew no sin — how vividly it all recalls the death of Isaiah's Servant!

F. Delitzsch writes, 'All the references in the New Testament to the Lamb of God (with which the corresponding allusions to the passover are interwoven) spring from this passage in the book of Isaiah.' This is perfectly true. John the Baptist introduces Jesus as the supreme Lamb of God who bears away the sins of the world (John 1:29). Jesus concludes his work by recalling that this precise prophecy must be fulfilled in him and that it is about to take place in his death (Luke 22:37). Philip begins to explain to the Ethiopian the good news about Jesus from this very passage in Isaiah (Acts 8:32-33). Peter commends to his readers the worth of a redemption by a Lamb without spot and

defect (1 Peter 1:19). The twin themes of John's vision on Patmos are
the death of a Lamb slain before the foundation of the world and the
triumph of a Lamb who inevitably leads his people to victory (Rev.
13:8; 5:9-14). It is difficult to envisage any or all of these without seeing
behind them Isaiah's prophecy and, in the more distant past, the
Passover lamb.

The guilt offering

The spectacle of a silent, innocent, dying lamb demands further
explanation and Isaiah gives it. The prophet predicts of the Servant's
death that it will fulfil not only the death of the paschal lamb, but also
of the guilt offering as well. In this way, the sacrificial metaphor has
double emphasis. Two themes from the altar combine to give the
portrait dramatic effect. They also reveal the purpose behind the
suffering as the imagery deepens. Indeed, in a strange way, they not
only explain the Servant's death, but also vindicate it. There is both
satisfaction and prospect of future blessing in what takes place. The
Servant, cut off in his prime without descendants, will eventually see
his offspring. Failure is turned into success, barrenness into
fruitfulness. Isaiah predicts the death of the Messiah and the rich
harvest of life which follows it.

> 'Yet it was the Lord's will to crush him and cause him to suffer,
>   and though the Lord makes his life a guilt offering,
> he will see his offspring and prolong his days,
>   and the will of the Lord will prosper in his hand.
> After the suffering of his soul,
>   he will see the light (of life) and be satisfied'
>
> (Isa. 53:10-11).

The description of the Servant's death as 'a guilt offering' calls for
reflection. Each of the Old Testament sacrifices had its own particular
emphasis. The burnt offering or holocaust stressed the total destruction
of the victim as an offering to God. The grain offering recalled how the
first fruit of the land might be offered. The peace or fellowship offering
spoke of reconciliation. The sin offering sought forgiveness from God.
The guilt offering attempted recompense to both God and man for
wrong-doing. The last two, the sin offering and the guilt offering, were
expiatory — that is, their purpose was to expiate, cancel or appease the
crime of sin against God and one's neighbour.

Of these two expiatory offerings, however, there were features
about the guilt offering which made it a particularly apt description of

the Servant's death. In the case of the sin offering, the victim could vary but in the case of the guilt offering it was always the same, a ram or male sheep. The choice of animal and the ritual followed were not in the slightest affected by the condition of the one who offered the guilt offering; it was uniform, unlike the sin offering. The sin offering was the oblation of the congregation, the guilt offering that of the individual. Above all, the idea of compensation, or the paying of a debt, was associated with the guilt offering.

The law was quite specific about such restitution, requiring one-fifth in addition to what was originally due. In the guilt offering the priest represented God, whereas in the sin offering he represented the people. The guilt offering spoke in a unique way of a compensation or restitution due to God because of sin. In the guilt offering the debt of sin is paid and restitution effectively made. It is for this reason that Anselm, the medieval theologian, described the fundamental emphasis of Christ's atonement as a satisfaction offered to God on behalf of sinners, a 'vicarious satisfaction'. This view has behind it the full weight of Isaiah 53:10.

The centrality of this doctrine

Of course, Christ's sacrifice fulfils all the varied features of Old Testament sacrifices. He offered himself up as a total oblation. His self-giving was a complete consecration. Through his death he provides reconciliation with God for his people. By his death he brings sinners forgiveness. But above all, Christ's sacrifice makes satisfaction. He expiates the crime of our sin by substituting himself for us as a sacrifice. This more than makes up for all our sins before God. His offering makes total restitution, cancels effectively the enormity of our debt, satisfies the justice of God his Father in full. Anselm was right. Christ's sacrifice was a vicarious satisfaction.

The New Testament makes the realization of this explicitly clear. It does so by disclosing the death of Christ at its deepest intensity as a sacrifice. When Jesus continues his teaching about his death, begun at Cæsarea Philippi, he climaxes it with a statement recalling Isaiah 53: 'For even the Son of Man did not come to be served, but to serve, and to give his life as a ransom for many' (Mark 10:45). The Messiah dies as a ransom. When Paul explains the source of the new birth and of reconciliation to the Corinthians, he has expiatory sacrifice particularly in view: 'God made him who had no sin to be sin for us, so that in him we might become the righteousness of God' (2 Cor. 5:21). The Messiah died as a sin offering. When the writer to the Hebrews stresses the superiority of Christ's self-offering over the animal sacrifices of

Judaism, his language is unequivocally plain: 'How much more, then, will the blood of Christ, who through the eternal Spirit offered himself unblemished to God, cleanse our consciences from acts that lead to death, so that we may serve the living God!' (Heb. 9:14). The Messiah dies as mediator of the new covenant. Peter, as we have already seen, explains the sacrificial nature of Christ's death specifically from Isaiah's prophecy (1 Peter 2:21-24). All of these, recalling the sacrifices of the Old Testament, emphasize Christ's death as a sacrifice for sin.

For this reason, it is sad to see how many shy away from this view of the atonement. It is too crude, unworthy of the dignity of Jesus' death, irrelevant to modern man's thinking and casts God in the role of a vindictive, unloving deity, they maintain. But surely this is the scriptural view of the Messiah's death, prophesied in the Old Testament, fulfilled in the New. Christ's death as a sacrifice pervades the Bible, not just figuratively, but actually. As a central act of her worship, Jesus commands the church to remember his broken body and shed blood (Matt. 26:26-28). Paul reminds the Ephesian elders that the church of God has been purchased by God's own blood (Acts 20:28). Peter writes of Christ's blood as precious, like that of a lamb without blemish or defect (1 Peter 1:19). John praises a triumphant Christ who loves us and has freed us from our sins by his blood (Rev. 1:5). Sacrificial atonement stands at the very centre of New Testament revelation.

The personal aspect of Christ' sacrifice

The personal aspect of this sacrificial death must also be recognized. It is basic to the entire argument of the writer to the Hebrews. The priest is also victim. The repeated animal offerings of the temple give way to the final, personal sacrifice of Jesus. Jesus himself had made this clear. The Good Shepherd dies for the sheep. In this way he becomes the door into the fold. When Paul and John describe Christ's death as a 'sacrifice of atonement' they bring us to the very heart of the matter. Once a year the high priest went into the most holy place in the temple alone and there sprinkled the blood of a bull and of a goat on the covering seat of the ark of the covenant. It was there, God had said, on the covering seat between the two angel figures, that he would meet with Moses and give commands to his people (Exod. 25:22). There, on the covering seat, atonement was made. Both Paul and John use the word for the covering seat to describe Christ's death (Rom. 3:25; 1 John 2:2). This is expiation. The death of the victim covers over and cancels out the sins of the worshipper.

But there is more. This is also propitiation, for the sacrifice appeases God's wrath by satisfying divine justice. It is not the wrath of an irate God demanding his pound of flesh, squeezing mercy out of his suffering Son, but the love of a just God, satisfied with the meeting of justice and mercy on the cross. 'All this is from God, who reconciled us to himself through Christ and gave us the ministry of reconciliation: that God was reconciling the world to himself in Christ, not counting men's sins against them' (2 Cor. 5:18-19). The death of Christ is a vicarious satisfaction which expiates the crime of sin and propitiates the wrath of God.

Only such a view of the death of Christ fully recognizes the enormity of man's sin, the compatibility of God's justice with his love and the self-giving of the Son of God for our sins: 'Christ, our Passover lamb, has been sacrificed' (1 Cor. 5:7). 'Christ died for our sins according to the Scriptures' (1 Cor. 15:3). These twin themes blend in Isaiah's portrait of the Servant's suffering and death.

Salvation

A sense of triumph pervades the close of Isaiah's oracle. The dark hues of the portrait are suddenly relieved by the introduction of fresh colours. It is as though the sad picture has hung for years in a damp, dark room, only seen by candlelight. Now the blinds are drawn and, as shafts of light fall on the subject, it somehow looks different. Colours are seen in a new way. The purpose of the portrait becomes much more clear. Strangely, in the midst of the darkness of suffering, dawn breaks. More than that, it is through the horror of death that hope comes.

Satisfaction

Isaiah speaks of the Servant's satisfaction. It is the satisfaction of the Servant seeing his seed and having his days prolonged. This is unusual, for the Servant has been sharply cut off from the land of the living, like a man in his prime, with no descendants. We think of the dying soldier on the grime of battlefield, his flesh torn open, the pain unbearable. His whole life rushes before him — childhood, youth, marriage. What has life been all about? Is there any purpose to it? He has only recently been married. His wife is expecting their first child. Is there a God at all? A message comes to tell of the birth of his son. He is relieved. His name will live on. He dies satisfied. Is this Isaiah's meaning, a belated satisfaction in the wake of grief and disappointment? Not at all. It far exceeds that. It is the satisfaction of triumph, of vindication, of the excellence of a work completed and the rich results which follow: 'After the suffering of his soul, he will see the light (of life) and be satisfied' (Isa. 53:11).

Is it also the satisfaction of resurrection? Resurrection is not prominent in the Old Testament, but there are hints. Job is confident that, though worms destroy his body, yet in his flesh he will see God (Job 19:26). David affirms that God will not abandon his Holy One to the grave nor let him see decay (Ps. 16:10) and maintains that he will go to his dead child even though his dead child will not come to him (2 Sam. 12: 23). Is Isaiah predicting that the Servant's satisfaction includes resurrection and that through this, his purposes are triumphantly fulfilled? Isaiah may not, indeed, go as far as that, but the fulfilment of Christ's death and resurrection becomes the glorious reality of which Isaiah's words are but the shadow. 'This certainly involves a strange paradox — he has died yet he prolongs his days. We cannot avoid the conviction that this points forward to the death and resurrection of Christ,' writes H. C. Leupold.

The satisfaction is certainly the satisfaction of covenant fulfilment. The seed of the woman was to bruise the seed of the serpent. Abraham was to have a large seed, like the stars in the heavens, in whom all the earth would be blessed. Jacob's seed was to be like the sand of the desert. It would have been clear to Isaiah, as to any God-fearing Jew, that these were the covenant promises of God to his people. As Isaiah reflected on the shoot of Jesse sprouting from the stump of the felled oak, he would readily understand how God's Servant could see his seed and rejoice over it. Through his death, God's Servant would bring a rich harvest of blessing to God's people. That was the covenant satisfaction he deserved. That was part of the reason for his death.

Justification

Above all, however, the portrait, in its spirit of triumph, displays the purpose of the Servant's death in his people's experience. This has been the growing sense already behind the visual oracle. The reason for the Servant's substitution was precisely that of his people's sins. The rationale behind the Servant's sacrifice was the atonement of his people's sins. The purpose of the Servant's death was ultimately the vindication of his people through the forgiveness of their sins. The specific manner of that forgiveness is described as their justification. The end of the Servant's sin-bearing finds satisfaction in his people's justification. The Servant is substitute, sacrifice and Saviour of his people.

'He will see his offspring and prolong his days,
   and the will of the Lord will prosper in his hand.
After the suffering of his soul,
   he will see the light (of life) and be satisfied;
by his knowledge my righteous servant will justify many,
   and he will bear their iniquities'

(Isa. 53:10-11).

Justification is the specific way in which the results of the Servant's death come to his people. The righteous Servant will justify many. Justification is a legal term. To justify means to acquit, to declare innocent, to clear the accused of guilt. This idea was well known throughout the Old Testament. God was perceived as the Judge of his people. He acquits the righteous and condemns the wicked. He gives judgements for his people when they obey; he gives judgements against them when they sin. Abraham saw God as the just Judge who would not condemn the righteous along with the wicked (Gen. 18:25). Jephthah committed his case to God as sovereign Judge who would give the verdict for Israel and against the Ammonites (Judg. 11:27). David proclaims God to be the merciful Judge who will deal with his people by means of his covenant (Ps. 50:6). Isaiah extols Jehovah's greatness as the active Judge, Israel's Judge and King, or Law-giver (Isa. 33:22). But it is not simply that a few important leaders saw God in this light. The entire way in which God dealt with his people was in accordance with these principles.

The law of God was the bedrock of this system. The law was not simply a collection of cold, legal edicts of precise ceremonial requirements; the law was educational. The judgements of the law were instruction. Moses gave the law. The judges, in his time and later, administered it. The priests taught it. The wise men commented on it. The kings, who led the people in war, directed the people in peace through the law. The prophets, who so often are seen as being against the law, frequently indicted the people for crimes against God's law and recalled them unashamedly to obedience to it. God's verdict was incontrovertible. To be condemned by God was the curse of the covenant; to be justified by God was the unsurpassable blessing of covenant fellowship. Every Israelite knew that God was Judge and that his judgement was just and final.

Those who are justified

The remarkable thing here is that Isaiah predicts God's Servant as justifying sinners, the unrighteous, the wicked. The verdict of God goes in favour of those who should rightly be condemned. It is not simply that they are vindicated before their enemies, that God favours his people with victory and condemns their enemies by defeat.

Isaiah had already spoken on that subject:

'They will say of me, "In the Lord alone
  are righteousness and strength."
All who have raged against him
  will come to him and be put to shame.
But in the Lord all the descendants of Israel
  will be found righteous and will exult'

(Isa. 45:24-25).

Nor is it even that God's Servant will be vindicated before his enemies. That triumph is indisputable:

'He who vindicates me is near.
  Who then will bring charges against me?
  Let us face each other!
Who is my accuser?
  Let him confront me!
It is the Sovereign Lord who helps me.
  Who is he that will condemn me?
They will all wear out like a garment;
  the moths will eat them up'

(Isa. 50:8-9).

It is rather that those who are sinners, condemned and guilty, are declared innocent by God because of his Servant's action. They gain the verdict undeserved. The issue, furthermore, is not simply the affairs of life, their well-being in health, their victory in battle. The issue is their sin, their guilt before God, about which they themselves can do nothing. They receive covenant blessing in the place of sin's curse.

The problem, of course, is the justice of God. How can God remain just and justify the wicked? Does he simply ignore or wink at their sin? By no means. Here again, the purpose behind Isaiah's portrait comes to the fore. God's righteous Servant justifies many by dying in their place, by bearing their iniquities. It is precisely because the Servant is his people's substitute and sacrifice for sin that he is their Saviour from sin. The Servant is, and remains, righteous in all this. God is, and remains, just in the entire process. God is both just and justifier. Sin is punished, divine justice is satisfied, the sinner is justified. The Servant's death procures this.

The Servant's knowledge

'By his knowledge my righteous servant will justify many, and he will bear their iniquities' (Isa. 53:11). Knowledge is the precise way by which God's Servant justifies his people. In this, not only is the object of justification, in terms of the acquittal of the wicked, unique, but the method as well. It is neither through inherent goodness nor through meticulous observance of the law, but through knowledge that God's Servant justifies.

But is it through the Servant's own knowledge, or through his people's knowing the Servant, that this takes place?

In favour of the former is the fact that knowledge is represented equally as the qualification for the priestly, prophetic and regal callings. The priest's lips should keep knowledge (Mal. 2:7). Faithful teachers turn many to righteousness (Dan. 12:3). 'The Spirit of knowledge' is one of the endowments falling upon the shoot of Jesse (Isa. 11:2) and fulfilled in Jesus. 'No one knows the Son except the Father, and no one knows the Father except the Son and those to whom the Son chooses to reveal him' (Matt.11:27).

In favour of the latter is the fact that Isaiah later claims that all Zion's children will be taught by the Lord (Isa. 54:13), that Jesus affirms in fulfilment of this promise that only those so taught will come to him (John 6:44-45) and that Paul maintains that the faith by which men are justified comes only by hearing the Word of God (Rom. 10:17).

Of course, these need not be mutually exclusive alternatives. Calvin avers Isaiah's clarity whichever interpretation is adopted: 'I acknowledge that the word *[dagnath]* may be taken in an active or a passive sense, as denoting either "the knowledge of him" or "his knowledge". In whichsoever of these senses it is taken, we shall easily understand the Prophet's meaning.'

What, however, is meant by 'knowledge'? In the Old Testament, knowledge is not primarily intellectual, but practical. It is not so much the grasping of facts, as the experiencing of a person. Dealing with human relationships, knowledge, in Hebrew, expresses the intimacy of marriage. In the realm of salvation, it speaks of the covenant relationship. God knows Israel exclusively among the nations. God promises to his people a knowledge of himself both universal and intuitive. When Isaiah predicts that through his knowledge God's Servant will justify many, he expresses the climax of a holy God's covenant dealings with a sinful people. There is no greater blessing of grace, no finer result of the Servant's death, than the justification of wicked men in this gracious fashion.

Justification through faith

The gracious nature of justification is vital. It is not through obedience to the law, but through knowledge of the Servant that acquittal takes place. This in itself is momentous. The righteousness is reckoned to the wicked, not for any merit he has, for he has none, but because of the Servant and his righteousness.

The idea of grace, God's unmerited favour, was not strange to Hebrew ears. It lay at the very heart of the covenant. Sacrifices provided forgiveness only for unwitting infringements of the law, and not for intentional sins. The cult was not a substitute for obedience to God's law. But even sincere obedience to the law could not justify. That lay within the preserve of God's grace alone. Abraham believed God and it was accounted to him for righteousness (Gen. 15:6). He held on to the promises of God, whatever the circumstances, until eventually they were fulfilled. David expresses the joy of forgiveness as of one whose sins God has covered. To him God graciously did not impute sin (Ps. 32:2). In this way alone could the stain of his adultery be removed. Habbakuk, beset by sin within Israel and the fear of Chaldean supremacy without, had to learn that the just man lives by faith (Hab. 2:4). Isaiah teaches the same lesson when he discloses the ultimate purpose of the Servant's death. Justification through knowledge of the Servant is justification through faith.

One place in the New Testament where this is clearly seen is in Paul's letter to the Romans. Paul writes of justification by faith as though his letter was the building of which these Old Testament themes were the blueprint. The details are fascinating. The setting is indisputably that of the lawcourt. God is Judge. His wrath is vented against all mankind. His righteous judgement falls on the sinner. Yet there is hope. A righteousness from God, a righteousness apart from the law, comes to sinful mankind and offers a way of escape through Jesus Christ, by whom man is justified. God is both just and the justifier of him who believes in Jesus.

The terminology is legal. Man is guilty, silenced before God, held accountable in the dock of God's judgement, only acquitted through Jesus Christ. The word Paul uses for 'justify' means to declare, rather than to make, righteous.

The argument flows as in a courtroom. Heathen man is condemned; having the light of God in nature, he sins against it. Thinking man is condemned; having the law of God written on his conscience, he ignores its warnings and goes his own way. Even religious man stands guilty. The Jew who declaims stealing, adultery and idolatry is too often guilty himself. All mankind is indicted before a holy God. Old

Testament texts substantiate the case. Habbakuk's affirmation, 'The righteous will live by faith' (Hab. 2:4) introduces the sequence. A chain of words from the psalmist convinces fearful man of his guilt. One link in the chain comes from Isaiah:

> 'Their feet are swift to shed blood;
> ruin and misery mark their ways,
> and the way of peace they do not know'
> (Rom. 3:15-17; cf. Isa. 59:7-8).

At this point, Isaiah has been complaining about the sad state of God's people, but in a markedly legal way. Justice and righteousness are distant and do not reach the people. Sins and offences are many in God's sight. There is no one to intercede, so God brings near his own righteousness (Isa. 59:9-16). Abraham's credited righteousness and David's discounted sin complete Paul's argument (Gen. 15:6; Ps. 32:1-2). Guilty man is acquitted through Christ's righteousness. Christ's righteousness is reckoned, or imputed to him.

What stands out most, however, is the way in which the death of Christ is at the very heart of this whole process of justification. It is through faith in Jesus' blood, whom God presented as a sacrifice of atonement, that enslaved man is redeemed from sin and guilty man is acquitted before God. This is how God is just and the justifier of the man who has faith in Jesus (Rom. 3:23-26).

The link between the death of Christ and justification and the acquisition of justification through faith in Christ, which Paul teaches, immediately recalls Isaiah's words: 'By his knowledge my righteous servant will justify many, and he will bear their iniquities' (Isa. 53:11).

The sin-bearing death of God's Servant makes justification possible. Justification, which comes through knowledge of God's Servant, is justification by faith. It is completely gratuitous. It comes as a gift from God offered through God's Servant, not through God's law. Isaiah not only predicts a justification which comes as a result of the death of the Servant; he prescribes clearly the way in which this justification is to be gained. Isaiah anticipates all that Paul affirms of a justification by grace through faith in Jesus' death.

The sovereign character of justification

It is the sovereign character of justification, as predicted by Isaiah and proclaimed by Paul, which grips the mind. God brings his righteousness near to his sinful people and makes it obtainable through the Servant's death. Who can condemn? It is God who justifies.

Moreover, Christ has died and risen again. He was delivered up for our offences, raised again for our justification (Rom. 8:34; 4:25).

The Catechisms of the Westminster Assembly stress this sovereignty in a clear way in their definitions of justification and sanctification. Justification is 'an act', sanctification 'the work' of God's free grace. In justification, God acts alone; in sanctification, man is involved. Justification is instantaneous, sanctification progressive. These definitions were shaped on the battlefield of the Reformation. Roman Catholic dogma taught an infused justification, begun at baptism and developed through life. Protestants maintained an imputed justification, a righteousness credited to the sinner's account, the result of repentance and faith, continued in a life of practical godliness. These definitions need to be recalled today.

The legal context of justification is essential to its meaning. To justify means to *declare*, not to make, righteous. Those opposing this view suggest that it implies a 'legal fiction'. It is, they say, defective because it is legal rather than relational, cultic rather than covenantal, to do with law not grace. But this is surely to miss the point! The whole legal aspect is clearly identifiable in both Old and New Testaments. Justification does not oppose the law; it answers the law. It meets the problem of the law's demands. It is both real and relational, for it affects man's standing before God. Through justification, man's status is changed from guilt to acquittal, from condemnation to innocence, and this charge is effected by a sovereign act of God's free grace. God's unconditional love, which lies behind his free, unmerited favour, makes justification possible. This removes the 'coldness' from the mere legality of the courtroom.

'Justification is an act of God's free grace, wherein he pardoneth all our sins, and accepteth us as righteous in his sight, only for the righteousness of Christ imputed to us, and received by faith alone' (*Shorter Catechism*, 33).

The joy of justification

The joy of justification is the other feature which is prominent in both Isaiah and Paul. The gloom of Isaiah's portrait is lightened by this truth. Defeat is turned into victory, darkness into light, failure into success. This atmosphere of triumph pervades the close of Isaiah's oracle as it does the writings of Paul: 'There is now no condemnation for those who are in Christ Jesus, because through Christ Jesus the law of the Spirit of life set me free from the law of sin and death' (Rom. 8:1-2).

We need to recover this in the Christian experience of conversion. It is part of the believer's 'religious affections'. Nowhere is it better expressed than in Count von Zinzendorf's hymn:

Jesus, thy blood and righteousness
My beauty are, my glorious dress;
Midst flaming worlds in these arrayed
With joy shall I lift up my head.

Bold shall I stand in thy great day
For who aught to my charge shall lay?
Fully absolv'd through these I am
From sin and fear, from guilt and shame.

When from the dust of death I rise
To claim my mansion in the skies,
Even then, this shall be all my plea:
Jesus hath lived, hath died for me.

Jesus be endless praise to thee,
Whose boundless mercy hath for me—
For me a full atonement made
An everlasting ransom paid.

Oh, let the dead now hear thy voice;
Now bid thy banished ones rejoice,
Their beauty this, their glorious dress
Jesus, thy blood and righteousness.

Isaiah puts the finishing touches to the portrait. In sweeping brush-strokes and tinted etching he highlights his message. The Suffering Servant is now the victor dividing the spoils of battle. He has a place among the greats in the hall of triumph. By his death he is a sacrifice who makes atonement, a substitute who identifies with sinners and a Saviour who justifies his people. There is one to intercede (cf. Isa. 59:16).

'Therefore I will give him a portion among the great,
    and he will divide the spoils with the strong,
because he poured out his life unto death,
    and was numbered with the transgressors.
For he bore the sin of many,
    and made intercession for the transgressors'

(Isa. 53:12).

6.
The gospel of Christ

Isaiah's Servant Songs move to their sad and yet glorious triumph. The prophet continues to detail the Messiah's victory. Jerusalem's future glory is assured. The place of her tent is enlarged. Her Maker is her husband (Isa. 54). Jerusalem's present satisfaction is proclaimed. The thirsty drink at the waters. Rich growth fills the land (Isa. 55). Jerusalem's past heritage includes the nations. The foreigner joins himself to the Lord. The eunuch is no longer a dry tree (Isa. 56). Victory is everywhere in the air. The place of honour which God's Servant has been given in the hall of fame is plainly evident. Christ's work and death inevitably lead to Christ's gospel. Good news is the order of the day.

The paradoxes of the gospel

The gospel, however, is a strange gospel. It is full of paradoxes, apparent contradictions. The element of mystery pervades. Isaiah's announcement arrests, startles and provokes thought. A profusion of joyful images tumble into the minds of his hearers, but they beg many questions. A sense of gladness is plain; how to gain it, beguiling. The method is easy, delightfully simple. The results are amazing, almost unbelievable in their magnitude. Can the news really be so good? Isaiah 55 records Christ's gospel.

The same is true in the New Testament. There the word is 'mystery'. The Greek religions had their mysteries. Only the initiated were admitted to the secrets. The word implied a closed society, a secret sect, a covert lodge. But the gospel mystery meant more than that. It was an 'open secret', an age-old plan eventually disclosed. That brought an air of excitement along with intrigue. When Jesus taught in parables, it was so that his disciples, and not outsiders, would enjoy the secrets of the kingdom. When Paul wrote of the mystery of the gospel, it was not that believers should grope in the darkness among the rites of their religion, but that God's eternal plan of salvation would be made clear. When John explained the meaning of his visions on Patmos, it was so that all would see the greatness of Jesus the King. The mystery of the apostolic gospel of the New Testament is so like the paradox of the prophetic gospel of the Old.

As Isaiah unfolds the paradox of Christ's gospel he reveals a strange pattern. It is as though the prophet is looking back to the Exodus, recalling all the wonder of those events, whereby God had rescued his people from Egyptian slavery by a strong arm and outstretched hand. The events, however, form the prelude to the 'second exodus', when God brought his people back from Babylon to their homeland. When Isaiah spoke, those events lay a century and a half in the future. Yet these are the things he obviously has in view. The good news is the story of the end of the exile, of Jews making their way back to Jerusalem. The migration that had taken place some fifty years earlier, in 587 B.C., was dramatically reversed. God's people returned to the land of promise.

The prophecy does not exhaust itself there. That rarely happens. There were future points of fulfilment. Timeless truths and principles were locked up in Isaiah's words, of which the exodus in the past, and the return from Babylon in the future, were only tokens. The good news ultimately looked forward to Christ's coming, his proclamation of the kingdom of God and the realization of that kingdom in the lives of those who submitted to him. In Christ, all the promises of God find their completion. Christ is the yes and amen to all God says. Isaiah's oracle predicts the gospel of Jesus the Messiah — deliverance from sin, satisfaction of life, a covenant relationship with God, a new nature and a growing transformation of existence. These are the eternal truths of Isaiah 55. They burst the bounds of redemption from Egypt and Babylon, overspill to the realities of Bethlehem and Golgotha and present their message in the haunting intrigue of paradox, the mystery of the gospel.

Free offer

The first paradox is the free offer of the gospel.

> 'Come, all you who are thirsty,
>   come to the waters;
> and you who have no money,
>   come, buy and eat!

Come, buy wine and milk
without money and without cost'

(Isa. 55:1).

Isaiah calls the people to satisfaction. The thirsty are to quench their thirst at the waters. The call is universal. He calls all of them and each of them. The only qualification is that they recognize their need and admit to thirst. The call is to richness. Water, wine and milk are more than simply the commodities of a staple diet. Israelite prosperity had always anticipated the prospect of each man under his own vine and fig-tree. There, he could rest in the shade in the heat of the day, luxuriate in the security of the fruitfulness around him. Wine would gladden his heart, olive oil would make his face shine, bread would sustain his bodily needs (Ps. 104:15). From milk would come curds, butter and cheese. Wine mixed with milk provided a delicacy for his meal. But he would know as he listened to Isaiah that all of these were symbols of a deeper reality, a richer satisfaction than mere bodily well-being. The law was clear about that. Man was not to live by bread alone, but by every word which came from God's mouth (Deut. 8:3).

What would grip him most about Isaiah's words, however, was that all of this was free. The offer is free, yet it can be bought, procured, just as at the market the foodstuffs were daily procured. There money was needed. Here it was different: this rich satisfaction, open to all and each who needed it, was on free offer. This was incredible.

God's provision in the wilderness

God's grace had always been that way for his people. No sooner had the memory of slave-masters in the brick-fields faded and the parted waters of the Red Sea become a thing of the past, than these discontented Jews complained to Moses and longed for the leeks, garlic and melons of the old life in Egypt. How much they missed them! Yet God provided for his people's needs: water from the rock, quails in the air, manna on the ground. They spent no money throughout their entire time in that endless Sinai desert. Yet their clothes never wore out nor did their ankles swell. The day after they arrived in Canaan, a land flowing with milk and honey, the manna ceased and they ate the fruit of the land. They ate the fruit of vines and fig-trees they had not planted, lived in houses they had not built and enjoyed the benefits of a land their generation had never ploughed.

The whole purpose of the manna was that they might realize a higher order of existence, God's words as food for their souls: 'He humbled you, causing you to hunger and then feeding you with manna, which neither you nor your fathers had known, to teach you that man does not live on bread alone but on every word that comes from the mouth of the Lord' (Deut. 8:3). However, both in the desert and in the homeland they forgot this. In their grumbling dissatisfaction, they missed the free offer of God's grace. The paradox was lost on them.

The exiles in Babylon

The paradox of free grace continued at the time of the exile. To a Jew in Babylon any suggestion of the ease with which the people would return to their homeland would have been unbelievable. In the midst of their troubles, Isaiah's words of satisfaction and prosperity would have seemed at best grossly irrelevant, at worst cruelly mocking or hurtfully insulting. The only waters they knew were those long canals cutting across the Babylonian landscape. Near these, they would meet for worship, hang their harps on the willows and listen to the taunts of their oppressors jibing at them about their God. Everywhere around them was fruitfulness, as in the hanging gardens, with their rich variety of plants and trees. But always the sinister presence of false gods, such as the stone ziggurat to Marduc with its steps reaching to heaven, stared them out of countenance and reminded them that they were a strange people in a strange land. Some of their fellow-countrymen had fared well, but their loyalty was suspect. As a people, they would have preferred distant Jerusalem, surrounded by its vine-clad hills, cut deep with ravines and valleys, inferior in size and fertility to these rich Babylonian plains. As to water, wine and milk, there was an abundance of these around them, but to talk of enjoying them, let alone enjoying them freely, was a nonsense. What did slaves know of free satisfaction? When things eventually did change and they were allowed to return to the waters, the wine and the milk of Jerusalem, it was an incredible display of free grace that was unimaginable in their present circumstances. Yet Isaiah had testified to that free offer a century and a half earlier.

The gift of eternal life

I remember early in my ministry visiting a lady who was interested in becoming a Christian. She grasped the meaning of the gospel, but was hesitant because of its simplicity. Could it really be so easy? Was it simply a matter of accepting a free gift? I suppose we all react that way to free offers. The extravaganza holiday, the bonanza prize, even the bargains in the supermarket, fill us with suspicion. If it is free, it must be cheap, we think. You only get what you pay for. There must be a catch. I took a Bible that was lying nearby and suggested to her that we think of it as a gift from her husband. He wanted her to benefit from it, to enjoy it and to gain pleasure from it. To offer him money for the Bible would be an insult. It was his gift to her. By its nature it was not to be bought, simply received. Yet she had to take it in order to benefit from it, to make it her own and read it with interest. She struggled for hours with that concept of the free gift. I called later and was glad to learn that she had made salvation her own. She went on to know great satisfaction from the gift she received that day, 'without money and without cost'. The puzzle was solved, the paradox became a reality.

Paul was astounded at the attitude of some members of the church at Rome. Were they really serious when they talked about going on sinning so that grace might increase? What a denial of their Christian faith! They were united to Christ in his death and resurrection, dead to sin, alive to righteousness. They were grafted into Christ and the strain of his holiness should have been transforming their character. To talk like this was lunacy. Part of their problem was that they had little notion of the slavery of sin from which Christ had set them free. Once they were slaves to sin. That meant increasing wickedness leading to death. Now they were slaves to God. That involved holiness resulting in eternal life. On an even deeper level, they had failed to grasp the difference in nature between those two ways of life. One was a drudgery with tragic results, the other a free offer with glorious consequences, 'For the wages of sin is death, but the gift of God is eternal life in Christ Jesus our Lord' (Rom. 6:23). Free grace, procured and enjoyed by receptive faith, is an integral part of the mystery of the gospel.

Whether for Jews fleeing from Egypt or returning from Babylon, or for first-century Christians at Rome, the timeless truth of Isaiah's words persists. The paradox and mystery of Christ's gospel is that it is a free offer which must be made our own by faith. We drink deeply of the water of life which Christ offers and know endless satisfaction. More than that, it springs up in us like a gushing well and flows to others. But the glory of it is that it is a free gift.

> I heard the voice of Jesus say,
> 'Behold I freely give
> The living water; thirsty one,
> Stoop down and drink, and live.'
> I came to Jesus, and I drank
> Of that life-giving stream;
> My thirst was quenched, my soul revived,
> And now I live in him.
>
> (Horatius Bonar)

Effortless work

Another paradox of Christ's gospel, according to Isaiah, is that it is effortless work.

'Why spend money on what is not bread,
    and your labour on what does not satisfy?
Listen, listen to me, and eat what is good,
    and your soul will delight in the richest of fare'

(Isa. 55:2).

As Isaiah continues, he addresses the problem of dissatisfaction. He questions the people's way of life. It brings neither lasting peace nor contentment. However, this is not a simple, but a complex problem. God's people lack no resources. There is sufficient money to purchase food. Nor is effort absent. They work from dawn to dusk. But as they expend both currency and energy, they never seem to get anywhere. There is no satisfaction. This is a frustrating problem. The student who neglects his work fails the examination, but understands the reason. The keen scholar who takes to his books, spends hours on his subject and still fails, is devastated. It seems so unjust. Something is obviously wrong.

Isaiah's message is a corrective. The problem is neither the resources nor the effort, but the commodity. The difficulty lies in the object to which all this energy and expense are directed. The bread is not worth it all, for it does not satisfy. The answer is not to labour, but to listen; not to work, but to wait; not to be endlessly active, but thoughtfully contemplative. God's people are on the wrong track. They are barking up the wrong tree. The paraphrase puts it well:

How long to streams of false delight
Will ye in crowds repair?
How long your strength and substance waste
On trifles, light as air?

My stores afford those rich supplies
That health and pleasure give:
Incline your ear, and come to me;
The soul that hears shall live.

(Scottish Paraphrases)

Isaiah is quite emphatic about this answer. He uses a strong expression: 'Hear by hearing.' Once again there is an element of paradox: there is bread and food to be had, but it is to be obtained by listening, not labouring, a kind of effortless work.

The Exodus

God taught this lesson of grace at the time of the Exodus too. A new Pharaoh came to the throne who was not acquainted with Joseph. In his opinion these Jews had been becoming far too numerous. They were a potential threat to Egyptian authority. Subjugated races had been known to overthrow their overlords. The new Pharaoh had no intention of allowing this to happen. He put slave-masters over the Jews to oppress them with forced labour. He ordered the Hebrew midwives to kill the baby boys but leave the girls. When this failed, the boys were to be thrown into the river. Still the Jews increased. He was ruthless with their workload. They would have no more straw to bind the clay into bricks, but they were still to produce the same daily quota. This was literally the last straw! It was the most frustrating aspect of all they had to bear. Here they were, working hard and pushed to work yet harder, but getting nowhere in the end. They knew the depressing futility of endless, fruitless toil.

God liberated them from Egyptian slavery by an effortless work. The way of release was not through a Jewish revolt of arms headed up by Moses. They were forced to wait, not to work for their freedom. They had to wait through those anxious months when Pharaoh seemed to soften, but then became even harder towards them. They had to watch as they toiled in the brick-fields and those plagues swept across the Nile — blood, frogs, gnats, flies, livestock, boils, hail, locust, darkness. They were made to feel the lash of the taskmaster's whip grow heavier as the Pharaoh's resentment increased. They had to listen rather than labour for redemption: to listen in depression to Moses' pleadings with Pharaoh: 'Let my people go'; to listen in strange wonder to the details of the slaughtered lamb, the sprinkled blood, the rushed meal, the flight in darkness; to listen with bated breath to the waters blown back, feel the dry sea-bed underfoot yet hear the crash of the waves on their pursuers. God had worked, but they had waited, listened and obeyed. That was the saga of their escape. For them, it was an effortless work.

The return from exile

Haggai was among the first wave of captives to return from Babylon. They would never forget the elation of those early days, the gracious way in which God had broken their bondage and brought them home. Time passed, however, and in their prosperity they forgot God and his goodness. Life settled into a pleasant routine and they had time to spend on themselves, their homes, their country. But all was not well. Beneath the apparent prosperity a sourness spread. Haggai diagnosed their condition: 'Now this is what the Lord Almighty says: "Give careful thought to your ways. You have planted much, but have harvested little. You eat, but never have enough. You drink, but never have your fill. You put on clothes, but are not warm. You earn wages, only to put them into a purse with holes in it"' (Hag. 1:5-6).

It was the whole distressing, frustrating cycle all over again. They worked hard, spent all they had, but were no better off. There was no satisfaction. Haggai put his finger on the problem. God's house, begun fifteen years before, was left unfinished. Their own homes were decorated to perfection. Their priorities were wrong, so their work was cursed. They were going round in circles. They had forgotten the effortless work of God's grace which brought them out of Babylon. Worse than that, they had forgotten and relegated the God of grace to limbo. They must repent and make things right.

Christ's gospel

Christ's gospel is an effortless work, as far as man is concerned. That is the mystery and paradox of it. Good, respectable people spend years of their lives being resourcefully active and sincere, but miss this point. They are frustrated and dissatisfied. It seems so unjust to them. A gospel of effortless grace is a further irritant which only makes the situation worse. In reality, it is the solution. They are expending all their energy on something unworthy. They are working for salvation. Not only does this food bring no satisfaction; it is no real food at all. Working for salvation is like going to streams of false delight, wasting strength and substance on trifles. They need to wait, not to work, to listen rather than labour, to give careful thought, not endless activity, to life.

Paul teaches this lesson again and again. Many of the churches to which he wrote needed the same truth. His own fellow-countrymen, the Jews, caused him most concern in this respect. Religious people always do. In his letter to the Ephesians, Paul stresses this aspect vigorously, and their background was by no means Jewish. They were Gentiles, uncircumcised, excluded from Israel's citizenship, foreigners to the covenants of promise. Yet Paul identifies with them, dead in sins, with a worldly lifestyle, controlled by the devil, disobedient to God, pandering to a sinful nature. What power unifies self-righteous Jews with self-seeking Gentiles? It is the power of Christ and his gospel, a gospel which is not only a gift of God, but a work of God — not a work of man. For in this whole transaction man is powerless, he is dead, depraved and disobedient: 'For it is by grace you have been saved, through faith — and this not from yourselves, it is the gift of God — not by works, so that no one can boast. For we are God's workmanship, created in Christ Jesus to do good works, which God prepared in advance for us to do' (Eph. 2:8-10).

The intriguing thing here is that Paul uses two different words for works. Speaking of man's works he uses the Greek word *erga*, from which comes our English 'energy', the hard, sweated toil of human effort. God's work, or workmanship, is *poiema*, the creative activity of divine sovereignty. God's work is a 'poem', his activity in salvation sheer poetry. We do not work to save ourselves. Our mundane efforts can never achieve that. God speaks and it is done. He works in us. That saves us. There is, however, a place for 'good works' in God's saving purpose. Good works are the *result*, not the source, of salvation; the *fruit*, not the root, of faith.

'We cannot, by our best works, merit pardon of sin, or eternal life at the hand of God, by reason of the great disproportion that is between them and the glory to come and the infinite distance that is between us and God.' 'These good works, done in obedience to God's commandments, are the fruits and evidences of a true and lively faith' (*Westminster Confession,* ch. 16:5, 1).

Isaiah proclaimed the paradox of an effortless work. It was evident in the exodus and exile, fulfilled in Christ and vibrant in Paul's gospel. The paradox and mystery continue.

A strange leader

Isaiah speaks of the paradox of a strange leader.

> 'Give ear and come to me;
>> hear me, that your soul may live.
> I will make an everlasting covenant with you,
>> my faithful love promised to David.
> See, I have made him a witness to the peoples,
>> a leader and commander of the peoples.
> Surely you will summon nations you know not,
>> and nations that do not know you will hasten to you,
> because of the Lord your God,
>> the Holy One of Israel,
>> for he has endowed you with splendour'

(Isa. 55:3-5).

The first unusual feature about this leadership is that it comes from outside the people themselves. They do not produce their own leadership. It comes from God. Not only must they stop working and listen to what God is saying to them; they must come to God. They must leave what they are doing, abandon their own pursuits, indeed, desert themselves, in order to come to God and hear what he has to say. This is the only way that their souls will live.

The covenant with David

The second strange thing about this leadership is that it comes through a Davidic Messiah, not by force of arms, but by covenant. It is not the military prowess of a warlord, but the spiritual power of a treaty-relationship which will order the lives of God's people. This calls for reflection. Isaiah had already predicted a coming Davidic King. The Messiah would rule on the throne of Judah for ever (Isa. 9:7). A shoot from the stump of Jesse would spring forth mightily under the power of the Spirit (Isa. 11:1-3). Isaiah had also mentioned a covenant. The Servant of the Lord would be a covenant for God's people (Isa. 42:6). Here he combines both ideas. A Davidic King would establish God's covenant with the people, but would do this in such a way that, as Isaiah's earlier prophecies had inferred, this kingdom would not ultimately be a return to the prosperous days of David at some future point in time, but an eternal kingdom. This King would rule over an everlasting kingdom by means of an everlasting covenant. There was an eternal and spiritual dimension to Isaiah's prophecy.

Other prophets also mention this. Hosea predicts a Davidic King in the last days (Hosea 3:5). Jeremiah heralds a Branch from David growing up in righteousness (Jer. 33:15-18). Ezekiel proclaims a shepherd and prince of the line of David, in whose time God will establish an everlasting covenant with his people (Ezek. 37:24-26). Events at the time of the exile, as the prophets of that day foretold, spelled out the end of the political kingdom of Judah. Jeconiah was exiled to Babylon. His successor Zedekiah was a mere puppet of Nebuchadnezzar. There would be no more king in Judah until one would come whose right to the throne was unassailable, for God would give it to him (Jer. 22:30; 2 Chron. 36:10; Ezek. 21:27). Only a spiritual seed of David remained, a mediator of an everlasting covenant to come.

Isaiah drives these spiritual truths home forcefully. God will 'cut' — a technical term for treaty-making — an everlasting covenant with his people. It will be characterized by the firmness of God's promises to David and confirmed by the Messiah as witness. In this capacity, he will lead and direct the people. The Messiah will be a covenant mediator.

The inclusion of the Gentiles

The third unusual feature of the leadership was that it would extend beyond the borders of Judaism. Gentile nations would be summoned by this new Israel under her new leadership. Of course Isaiah, among others, had already hinted at that. Not only would the root of Jesse stand as a banner for the peoples gathering exiles home, but Egypt would be called God's people, Assyria God's handiwork and Israel God's inheritance (Isa. 11:10,12; 19:25). The Servant would be both a covenant for Israel and a light for the Gentiles (Isa. 49:6). Isaiah here depicts nations running in glad acknowledgement to Israel and her leader. Unknown nations will be included in the people of God.

Moses

When we think of it, Moses' leadership at the time of the Exodus was strange. It also had a unique quality about it. There were features about Moses which admirably suited him for his task: his survival at birth, his Egyptian education in Pharaoh's court, his personal courage to stand alongside his own people. Yet he was all too conscious of his own deficiencies: 'Who am I to go to Pharaoh? Suppose they do not listen to me. I am no speaker.' But God used him, and he did so in a unique way. God spoke with Moses as a man with his friend, face to face. With no others did God do this. When Aaron and Miriam attempted this intimacy, God judged them fiercely. Moses went to the tabernacle; the Israelites stood at their tents. God spoke to Moses, then Moses spoke to the people. Moses ascended the smoking Sinai, received the tables of the law and brought them to the people. Moses gave the details of the Passover meal, directed the Exodus, countered the grumbling, judged the disputes, and led in the desert, because Moses had first listened to God. Moses mediated between God and the people. The extraordinary nature of Moses' leadership rested not on his personal expertise, or diplomacy, but on a close covenant-like relationship with God. It would be a prophet like Moses whom God would eventually raise up to whom his people must listen. If they did not, they would die. Moses' leadership was undoubtedly unique.

Cyrus

What was true of the Exodus, was true of the exile. When Isaiah forecast the return from Babylon, it lay in the distant future. In Isaiah's day, the details would have been hazy, indistinct, even irrelevant. The mention of a certain Cyrus would not even have raised an eyebrow. How

different it was in 538 B.C.! The suddenness with which Cyrus
overthrew Babylon without striking a serious blow, the favour he
showed to the Jews, allowing them not only to return and carry with
them the sacred vessels, but actually encouraging them to rebuild the
ruined temple in Jerusalem, made Isaiah's prophecy live.

Isaiah had predicted Cyrus by name, described him as God's
shepherd, indeed God's messiah, and specifically referred to the
rebuilding of the temple (Isa. 44:28; 45:1). This was incredible. God
was making the wrath of man to praise him and forecasting it a century
and a half before it happened. God had used Joseph to bless the Jews
in Egypt. That was one thing. This was quite different. God had
appointed a Persian king as his people's messiah. Such leadership was
paradoxical beyond belief. The decree of Cyrus embodies this truth:
'The Lord, the God of heaven, has given me all the kingdoms of the
earth and he has appointed me to build a temple for him at Jerusalem
in Judah. Anyone of his people among you — may the Lord his God be
with him, and let him go up' (2 Chron. 36:23; Ezra 1:2-3).

Salvation from Babylonian exile was by God's anointed through
God's covenant decree. Isaiah had predicted this with amazing clarity.

The fulfilment in Christ

The paradox of leadership finds its fulfilment in Jesus. Again, it is the
unusual feature of leadership which is to the fore. Jesus comes from the
obscurity of a carpenter's home in Nazareth. He identifies in a common
cause with the somewhat eccentric John the Baptist. He gathers a few
poor and ill-educated followers around him. He refuses kingship when
the offer arises. He will not go public on the subject of his messiahship.
He insists, with growing seriousness, on the necessity of his own death.
He teaches quite other-worldly principles and is content to encourage
his people to a reward in heaven. All of this, in public estimation, will
not impress. The people are glad of his healings, gape at his miracles,
but he is not of the stuff of which Jewish messiahs are made. So, at a
crucial point, many who once followed him desert the cause. When, in
the event, he suffers Roman crucifixion, he has blown his cause, missed
his opportunity and sinks into the oblivion which, in the opinion of
others, he justly deserves: he saved others; himself he cannot save.

Christians, however, see Christ's leadership very differently. To
them, it is unique. He is the God-man who chooses the way of the cross
and shame rather than the path of fame and glory. He goes that way of
necessity, in order to save mankind from sin. He does this by fulfilling
the covenant purpose of God. He is born because of the covenant with
the patriarchs, dies in the cause of the new covenant for the forgiveness

of sin, rises from death by the blood of the everlasting covenant (Luke 1:54-55; Matt. 26:28; Heb. 13:20-21). Christ is God's mediator of a new covenant, the King of a kingdom not of this world, a strange leader of a cause which not only transforms Jewry, but the Gentiles as well.

As Paul unfolds the mystery of Christ to Christians at Rome and Galatia he makes this point. Paul begins the leadership saga in this case, neither with Moses nor Cyrus, but with Abraham. Of Abraham, he says quite remarkable things. Abraham is justified by faith, receives the sign of this justification, which is circumcision, has the gospel of Christ preached to him in advance and is the father of all who believe, both circumcised and uncircumcised. Christ is the seed of Abraham to whom the promises were made. Christians are Abraham's seed and heirs according to promise. But above all, Paul writes these words which define so well Christ's covenant leadership of both Jews and Gentiles: 'Christ redeemed us from the curse of the law by becoming a curse for us, for it is written: "Cursed is everyone who hangs on a tree." He redeemed us in order that the blessing given to Abraham might come to the Gentiles through Christ Jesus, so that by faith we might receive the promise of the Spirit' (Gal. 3:13-14).

What Isaiah says of the strange type of leadership recalled in Moses and anticipated in Cyrus is gloriously fulfilled in Jesus of Nazareth. These words of Paul clinch the matter.

An immanent God

The fourth paradox is that of an immanent God, a God who is close at hand.

> 'Seek the Lord while he may be found;
>   call on him while he is near.
> Let the wicked forsake his way
>   and the evil man his thoughts.
> Let him turn to the Lord, and he will have mercy on him,
>   and to our God, for he will freely pardon.
> "For my thoughts are not your thoughts,
>   neither are your ways my ways,"
>
> declares the Lord'
(Isa. 55:6-8).

Sin separates man from God

Since the Fall, God had become distant from man. God had put Adam and Eve out of the garden. Angels, with a flaming sword flashing back and forth, guarded the tree of life. Man's re-entry was barred. Subsequent events reflected this estrangement. God would speak to man, but only sporadically, through visions, dreams, the angel of the Lord and, eventually, the table of the law, the oracles of the prophets and the proverbs of the wise men. Gone were the days of God speaking with man face to face in the cool of the day, in the shade of the garden. The lines of communication were effectively broken with the Fall.

Since the Fall, man had become distant from God because of sin. Sin had not only entered mankind; it had spread vigorously. John Murray puts it this way: 'The immediate sequel in the unfolding history of Adam's family is the catalogue of sins — envy, malice, hatred, homicide, polygamy, violence. "I have slain a man for wounding me and a young man for bruising me." "If Cain shall be avenged sevenfold truly Lamech seventyfold." "The wickedness of man was great within the earth, the earth was filled with violence, all flesh had corrupted its way upon the earth."'

The climax of this process is described in Genesis 6:5: 'The Lord saw how great man's wickedness had become, and that every inclination of the thoughts of his heart was only evil all the time.' The language is intense. The first stirrings of man's thinking process focus on evil. His behaviour follows suit. Sin is instinctive, exclusive, continual and pervasive in man's nature. Man's thoughts and ways are evil.

Above all, sin has separated man from God, for God's thoughts and ways are good. So Adam and Eve hid from God's presence, Moses was protected from God's face, Manoah feared death through encountering God in human form and Isaiah felt devastated as he gazed on God's holiness. God was distanced from man and man from God. Their natures were incompatible, because they were opposites. Their thoughts and ways were poles apart. Not just their behaviour, but its motivation were entirely incongruous. The root cause was sin. Sin had separated God from man and man from God.

> '"For my thoughts are not your thoughts,
>   neither are your ways my ways,"
>
> declares the Lord.
>
> "As the heavens are higher than the earth,
>   so are my ways higher than your ways
>   and my thoughts than your thoughts"'
>
> (Isa. 55:8-9).

A God who is near

The problem seemed insurmountable, but it was resolved by God's grace. The gospel is a paradox. God solves the insoluble by taking the initiative. God, who has separated himself from man and has separated man from himself, draws near. The distant God comes close; the transcendent Creator is immanent. That is why the implications of Isaiah's challenge are incredible. Man, whose way is wicked, whose thoughts are evil, is to seek a God who may be found, to call on a God who is close and to turn to a God who will freely pardon. The answer to man's plight is not only that he may seek a God who has taken steps to restore fellowship with himself, but that he may find a God who will effectively deal with his sin. God can not only be found, but he is merciful, and man, as a consequence, can be pardoned.

The paradox is a double one. It speaks of a change of attitude on God's part which leads to a change of condition in man. God turns to man so that man might turn to God. The flaming sword flashing back and forth has been stayed. Man glimpses the tree of life because of God's mercy.

This truth was forecast at the burning bush. Moses was mystified as the bush burned, but did not burn up. His curiosity got the better of him. He went to examine it. His face drained and his curiosity turned to fear when the bush spoke. The angel of the Lord, the Lord, addressed him. He must take off his sandals; the ground was holy. The voice announced itself as the God of Abraham, Isaac and Jacob. The lines of communication were opened, but Moses was petrified. The voice continued: 'I have indeed seen the misery of my people in Egypt. I have heard them crying out because of their slave drivers, and I am concerned about their suffering. So I have come down to rescue them from the hand of the Egyptians and to bring them up out of that land into a good and spacious land, a land flowing with milk and honey' (Exod. 3:7-8).

God was not just near; God was merciful. God's mercy, moreover, was not just sympathetic emotion, an upsetting concern; it was active pity. God was going to do something about the situation. He would rescue his people from the Egyptians.

The most intriguing thing of all for Moses was the name of God, the authority by which he, Moses, was to approach Pharaoh about the matter. The God of Abraham, Isaac and Jacob was the I AM God. The Hebrew verb I AM has the same letters from which comes the title 'Jehovah', translated by the word LORD, written in capitals by the translators, to show its Hebrew origin. The name was the covenant title for God, the God who draws near to save his people from slavery and make them his very own. To this day, Jews will not repeat the sacred name of LORD, but substitute another title when reading the Scriptures aloud. Moses was authorized by the covenant God of Israel. Communication was restored. That was not all. God in mercy would redeem his people from slavery. That would be his name for ever.

Isaiah had already spoken of God's nearness in quite a remarkable way (Isa. 7:1-25). When Rezin, King of Aram, and Pekah, King of Israel, joined in confederacy to attack Jerusalem, Ahaz, King of Judah, and his people were filled with fear. God, as we have already seen, encouraged Ahaz through Isaiah. These two enemies were like smouldering stubs of firewood soon to be extinguished. Ahaz should ask a sign from God. Even when he refused to do so, on the grounds that it would involve putting God to the test, God gave him a sign. A virgin would have a boy. He would eventually feed on the best, on curds and honey. But before he reached the years of understanding the two enemies would be quashed. How that would happen would be uncanny. Egypt and Assyria would have a part to play. Indeed, Judah would do better to anticipate trouble from those quarters, not from Aram or from Israel. The curds and honey would be the exception, provided for by a lone man keeping a young cow and two goats. Elsewhere, instead of vines, the land would be covered with briers and thorns. It was a strange mixed comfort. Strangest of all was the boy's name. He would be called Immanuel. It means 'God with us'.

God would be with his people in their time of trouble. He would identify with them and rescue them from their enemies, not merely the threat of civil strife from Aram and Israel, but foreign invasion from Assyria. The whole sequence was to be repeated at the exile over a hundred years later. The same strange and wonderful identification of God with his people took place. The intervention of a foreign power was the instrument of God's deliverance. Cyrus of Persia replaced Sennacherib of Assyria. The motivation of these events, as at the exodus and in Isaiah's day, was God's mercy, his active pity, his caring love in remembering his covenant with his people. The distant God drew near to identify and deliver because of the covenant oath he had sworn.

Ezekiel, predicting the return from exile, expresses tenderly yet firmly this concept of 'love to the loveless shown that they might lovely be' when he says, 'This is what the Sovereign Lord says: I will deal with you as you deserve, because you have despised my oath by breaking the covenant. Yet I will remember the covenant I made with you in the days of your youth, and I will establish an everlasting covenant with you. Then you will remember your ways and be ashamed... So I will establish my covenant with you, and you will know that I am the Lord' (Ezek. 16:59-62).

The incarnation

The New Testament is full of this aspect of the gospel: God identifying in nearness with mankind to rescue, redeem and save from sin. This is the theme of the incarnation. Matthew sees the Immanuel prophecy fulfilled in the birth of Jesus, a Jesus so called for he would save his people from sin (Matt. 1:21). John speaks of the Word becoming flesh so that people might receive the Word and be born of God (John 1:12-14). The writer to the Hebrews extols the virtues of a Christ who is like us in every way, sin excepted, not just as our sympathetic High Priest, but as a Saviour who atones for sin and delivers from death and the devil (Heb. 2:14-18).

Paul, who writes to Timothy and Titus to help them in their work, also reveals this mixture of miracle and mercy in the gospel of incarnation. The miracle is the motivation for godly living within God's household, the church of the living God, the pillar and foundation of the truth: 'Beyond all question, the mystery of godliness is great:

'He appeared in a body,
   was vindicated by the Spirit,
was seen by angels,
   was preached among the nations,
was believed on in the world,
   was taken up in glory'

(1 Tim. 3:16).

The mercy of God is the source of man's salvation: 'But when the kindness and love of God our Saviour appeared, he saved us, not because of righteous things we had done, but because of his mercy. He saved us through the washing of rebirth and renewal by the Holy Spirit, whom he poured out on us generously through Jesus Christ our Saviour' (Titus 3:4-6).

The lines of communication are open again. God has drawn near to man estranged from God through sin. God has heard man's cry because of sin's oppression, has had mercy on man's plight and has come down to deliver man. God is a God who may be sought, called upon and turned to, even by wicked, sinful man. For God is merciful and, though different from man as day from night, he has come near to save man. God is Immanuel; he is God with us. 'The Lord is near. Do not be anxious about anything' (Phil. 4:5).

An active word

The fifth paradox Isaiah mentions is an active word. This is the means or instrument by which the fellowship with God is restored and man's redemption through the gospel is effected. The gulf between sinful man and a holy God is bridged because of God's mercy. The deliverance which that mercy promises comes through God's Word.

God's Word brings about the deliverance because it is an active word. It is not something which is merely propositional, the statement of a principle. It is that, but it is more. It is a living statement, an authoritative pronouncement, a vital word. It is as sure in its effects in the spiritual realm as is rain upon the earth in the natural. God sends the rain from heaven. It waters the earth and produces the crop. It gives seed for the sower and bread for the eater. The process is not only life-giving; it is complete and effective. Rich results, in line with the divine purpose, issue from it. No philosophy of man can accomplish this. Human theories can have impressive results, but nothing comparable to this. This is what sets the Word of God apart from human tradition. This is what makes the Bible different from all other books. God's Word is alive, life-giving and effective. God's Word accomplishes the divine purpose.

> 'As the rain and the snow
>   come down from heaven,
> And do not return to it
>   without watering the earth
> and making it bud and flourish,
>   so that it yields seed for the sower and bread for the eater,
> so is my word that goes out from my mouth:
>   It will not return to me empty,
> but will accomplish what I desire
>   and achieve the purpose for which I sent it'
>
> (Isa. 55:10-11).

The Word active in creation

This truth is foundational. It goes back to the very beginning of things. God's work of creation was accomplished through his active word. God said and it was done. The panoramic view of creation in Genesis makes this clear (Gen. 1:1-31). Light, sky, sea, land, vegetation, sun, moon, stars, fish, birds, animals arise effortlessly at the mere word of God's command. Even the unique making of man comes from God's speaking. 'The work of creation is God's making all things of nothing by the word of his power in the space of six days, and all very good' (*Shorter Catechism,* 9). There was a perfection about all this. God's active word produced results, perfect results, totally in keeping with what God purposed. The language of the Old Testament reflects this.

The Hebrew *dabar*, which means 'word', can also be translated 'event'. God's word is an event, for it is eventful.

Man's abuse of God's law

The Fall distorted this perfect creation. It marred the image of God in man. It affected God's Word, not so much in its procession from God, as in its perception by man. Man, distanced from God by sin, now only heard God fitfully and unclearly.

The written law on Sinai was a great act of sovereign grace. God put his Word in writing. It was clear and precise. But sinful man abused it. He replaced it with a golden calf, transgressed it by his daily lifestyle, misconstrued its meaning to suit his own designs, made a fetish of it, shaped it into an idol through obedience to which he hoped to gain favour with God. That which was living and active became dead and deadening. Man's sin did this. Man broke the covenant law of God at Sinai.

The law, however, had not been given for such abuse. It was given to a covenant people by the Lord their God who had brought them up out of Egypt, out of the land of slavery. It was designed to direct and instruct, to mould and to shape their covenant life with God. It was meant to bring God actively near to them.

When the aged Moses was ready to go to his reward, he made the tribes of Israel recite the blessings and cursings of the law. Their choice must be to obey the life-giving Word which was near them: 'Now what I am commanding you today is not too difficult for you or beyond your reach. It is not up in heaven, so that you have to ask, "Who will ascend into heaven to get it and proclaim it to us that we may obey it?" … No, the word is very near you; it is in your mouth and in your heart so that you may obey it' (Deut. 30:11-14).

This was the norm, but it happened rarely enough in practice. Isaiah had already insisted on the authority of the law in the confused days of mediums and spiritists: 'To the law and to the testimony! If they do not speak according to this word, they have no light of dawn' (Isa. 8:20). Here, in Isaiah 55, he proclaims the life-giving power of God's Word of which he himself was a prophet.

The new covenant promised

Again, however, the fulfilment of this glorious principle had to wait in part for the days of the exile. It was Jeremiah who announced the vital role of this transforming law in the new covenant which God would make with Israel and Judah:

'"The time is coming," declares the Lord,
     "when I will make a new covenant
with the house of Israel
     and with the house of Judah.
It will not be like the covenant
     I made with their forefathers
when I took them by the hand
     to lead them out of Egypt,
because they broke my covenant,
     though I was a husband to them,"
                                                              declares the Lord.
"This is the covenant that I will make with the house of Israel
     after that time," declares the Lord.
"I will put my law in their minds
     and write it on their hearts.
I will be their God,
     and they will be my people.
No longer will a man teach his neighbour,
     or a man his brother, saying, 'Know the Lord,'
because they will all know me,
     from the least of them to the greatest,"
                                                              declares the Lord.
"For I will forgive their wickedness
     and will remember their sins no more"'
                                                              (Jer. 31:31-34).

What a glorious transformation! The law, God's Word, would be
active. It would be written on the minds of the people. A grace would
be given which would enable them to keep the law, unlike the situation
at Sinai — the grace of regeneration. Their knowledge of God would
not be by learning or by rote, but rather intuitive and intimate — not a
head, but a heart knowledge, regardless of social class or intellectual
ability. This effective establishment of the covenant would truly make
them God's people. The law written on their minds would do what the
law written on the stone tables could not do: their sins would be totally
forgiven.

The Word active in salvation

The New Testament celebrates this gospel principle of salvation from
sin through God's active Word. It is part of the paradox of the gospel.
Jesus gives his followers words from God through which they come to
believe in him as Messiah (John 17:8). John extols the virtues of the

living Word through whom men and women are born of God (John 1:12-14). James sees Christians as a kind of new species, issuing out of God's mouth by the word of his truth (James 1:18). Peter specifies the gospel of salvation as the imperishable word of God (1 Peter 1:24-25).

Paul describes the process in detail. Mankind is saved not by works of the law, but by the hearing of faith. Faith comes through hearing, hearing through the Word of God (Rom. 10:17). But he discerns the vitality of this, above all, in Timothy's life (2 Tim. 3:14-16). The Scriptures, which Timothy has known from childhood, are capable of making him wise about salvation through faith in Jesus the Messiah. All Scripture is God-breathed and so is effective for instruction, correction, warning and training. Timothy is living proof of this. God's Word has been active in his life — at home, in conversion and in service. He is a perfectly equipped young man.

Much evangelism today sadly lacks this dimension. Family worship is a dying, if not a dead phenomenon. Men and women are called to decide for Jesus in an emotional atmosphere devoid of biblical proclamation. The terrors of the law are unknown. The persuasiveness of the Word is a neglected process. Yet the preaching of the New Testament cries out against this. The sermons of Acts are biblical in structure and dynamically scriptural in their appeal, whether to Jew or Gentile. Not only evangelism, but teaching often lacks this quality. Christians are convinced by human experience, not by divine truth. We know little of the psalmist's experience of hungering for God's Word, meditating on it day and night, storing it up in our hearts, finding it sweeter than honey to our taste. Yet some question the regeneration of Old Testament saints. Isaiah is in no doubt as to the paradox of the active Word of God in the gospel of Christ. Nor should we be. Paul prays for the Thessalonians that the God of peace will sanctify them through and through, spirit, soul and body being kept blameless at the coming of the Lord Jesus Christ (1 Thess. 5:23). This is the fulfilment of the Old Testament demand to love the Lord with all the heart, soul, mind and strength. Totality of response is required — every aspect of our beings. Only obedience to God's Word will accomplish this.

'The Spirit of God maketh the reading, but especially the preaching of the word, an effectual means of convincing and converting sinners, and of building them up in holiness and comfort, through faith, unto salvation' (*Shorter Catechism*, 89).

A transformed land

The final paradox is a transformed land.

'You will go out in joy
    and be led forth in peace;
the mountains and the hills
    will burst into song before you,
and all the trees of the field
    will clap their hands.
Instead of the thornbush will grow the pine tree,
    and instead of briers the myrtle will grow.
This will be for the Lord's renown,
    for an everlasting sign,
    which will not be destroyed'

(Isa. 55:12-13).

Isaiah had spoken this way before. The blessings which God would eventually bring to his people would be accompanied by nature rejoicing on every side. Indeed, nature would have a vital role to play in that climax, not just as an accompaniment. The curse, which the Fall had laid on creation, would one day be removed. The desert would blossom like a crocus (Isa. 35:1-2). A way would be cleared through the scrubland (Isa. 40:3-4). Cedar, acacia, myrtle, olive, pine, fir, cypress would be the result of streams on parched ground (Isa. 41:7-20). Even wild animals would mellow in ferocity out of respect for God and his people (Isa. 35:9-10; 43:19-20).

All of this would not be an end in itself, but a means to smoothing out and easing the return of God's people to their homeland, a land of great fruitfulness and prosperity. Future prospects were full of that:

'Leave Babylon,
    flee from the Babylonians!
Announce this with shouts of joy
    and proclaim it.
Send it out to the ends of the earth;
    say, "The Lord has redeemed his servant Jacob."
They did not thirst when he led them through the deserts;
    he made water flow for them from the rock;
he split the rock
    and water gushed out'

(Isa. 48:20-21).

The first exodus anticipated a second. What God did once through nature to redeem from Egypt, he would do again in Babylon. There would be no doubt about that.

Isaiah here rings out a final song of these events. But he includes it in the gospel of Christ. These things are not confined to the exodus from Egypt or the return from Babylon: they point forwards to what God will do through his promised Messiah. The path back to God will be cleared so that his people might return to him. The blessing of God will be rich so that his people might enjoy him. The miracle of *redemption* is here. Led forth from enslaved conditions, they find that nature assists and applauds their escape. The miracle of *transformation* is present. Instead of scrubland, nettles and desert briers blocking their path and spoiling their inheritance, evergreen and fruitful myrtles cover the renewed landscape. The miracle of *perseverance* is theirs. Their future is guaranteed. These things are lasting testimonies to God's renown. When oriental kings returned from battle, they often carved their victory in rocks, a kind of permanent war memorial record. Other conquerors, however, would follow, smash these tablets to pieces and erect their own memorial plaques. Not so with God's redeeming and transforming grace. It persists and produces an unnatural and permanent growth of profuse proportions.

The land in the past

Isaiah, as ever, looks back to Egypt and forwards to Babylon, only here he does it in the context of the land. The land had always been important to God's people. It was a mark of their covenant relationship with God, a tangible token of his goodness to them and his lordship over them. From the very outset, when God promised the land to Abraham's offspring, the story begins. Sometimes that inheritance seemed unreal, as Abraham eyed the scrubland around Bethel and envied Lot's pastures near Sodom, or as Jacob trudged over the Jordan, lonely, fearful, with only his staff in his hand, or as Joseph lay embalmed in a coffin in Egypt. But God was always there, restoring them graciously to that land, and providing for them abundantly in it. The miracle of God's redeeming grace was constant, traced out in the paradox of a land which at one time his people had, and at another they had not, but of which, in the event, God granted them possession.

The Exodus replayed the theme. The rushed meal, the escape from Egypt, manna in the desert, water from the rock, a land flowing with milk and honey, houses they did not build, vines they did not plant, crops they did not sow — all were unforgettable features in the story. Not only the Passover, but the Feast of Tabernacles brought it all back to them: 'On the first day you are to take choice fruit from the trees, and palm fronds, leafy branches and poplars, and rejoice before the Lord your God for seven days... Live in booths for seven days: All native-born Israelites are to live in booths so that your descendants will know that I made the Israelites live in booths when I brought them out of Egypt. I am the Lord your God' (Lev. 23:40-43).

These were lasting signs of God's grace. God not only gave them a land; he brought them safely to it and blessed them lavishly in it. Was it any wonder the mountains would sing and the trees applaud?

Looking to the future

The return from exile was somewhat different, however. The similarities were undoubtedly there. It was, indeed, a second exodus. God's people were returning to their homeland. But in Moses' day, it was predominantly a fearful affair, with the surrounding darkness and the pursuing Egyptians. It was also a lengthy episode. Forty years they wandered through the Sinai peninsula until a whole sinful generation died. The return from Babylon was not quite the same. Great joy attended Cyrus' proclamation. A relaxed atmosphere filled the air. They made their way back in broad daylight assisted by the king's decree. There was not the same rush. It was over a space of a few years that the first and last of the exiles returned. There was no aimless wandering. They returned with joy and directness. In that sense, the second exodus was different.

Isaiah reflects this in his prophecies. He alludes to the water from the rock at the time of the Exodus, God's remarkable provision in a time of need. He advises leaving Babylon with shouts of joy, a jubilant exercise in a time of plenty (Isa. 48:20-21; cf. 55:11-12). The experience at the exile was one step nearer the realization in the gospel.

The gospel of Christ celebrates supremely this paradox of redemption, transformation and permanence: 'The creation waits in eager expectation for the sons of God to be revealed. For the creation was subjected to frustration, not by its own choice, but by the will of the one who subjected it, in hope that the creation itself will be liberated from its bondage to decay and brought into the glorious freedom of the children of God' (Rom. 8:19-21).

The transformation of human nature

What Paul says about the transformation and permanence which this redemption brings to mankind's nature strongly points up the paradox. Jesus had taught that Christians are branches in himself, the vine, bearing his strain, carrying his life, producing fruit (John 15:1-8).

Without this, they are nothing. By this, their genuineness is to be tested. Paul takes up the theme (Rom. 11:8-24). Branches have been broken off so that the Gentiles might be grafted in. Under the influence of the Spirit they bear fruit. The acts of the sinful nature give way to the fruit of the Spirit. The transformation is startling and permanent. This best illustrates the paradox of the gospel. The ultimate reality of a transformed land is not in the context of nature, but in human life and character: 'The acts of the sinful nature are obvious: sexual immorality, impurity and debauchery; idolatry and witchcraft; hatred, discord, jealousy, fits of rage, selfish ambition, dissensions, factions and envy; drunkenness, orgies, and the like. I warn you, as I did before, that those who live like this will not inherit the kingdom of God. But the fruit of the Spirit is love, joy, peace, patience, kindness, goodness, faithfulness, gentleness and self-control. Against such things there is no law. Those who belong to Christ Jesus have crucified the sinful nature with its passions and desires. Since we live by the Spirit, let us keep in step with the Spirit. Let us not become conceited, provoking and envying each other' (Gal. 5:19-26).

When that change occurs, mountains will sing and trees applaud. Indeed, creation itself will one day know this redemption, transformation and permanent change. The gospel will restore all that was lost in the Fall. Eden will be regained through Jesus the Messiah. This is the final and glorious paradox of the gospel of Christ which Isaiah predicts.

7.
Light for the Gentiles

Christ, as we have seen, appears in Isaiah in all his glory — his coming, kingdom, salvation, work, death and gospel. In the closing section of the prophecy, chapters 56-66, the scene is again somewhat different. It once more celebrates the return of the Jews from Babylon but here, as compared with chapters 40-55, the emphasis is on the homeland. Much corruption marks the homeland, for the people soon forgot God's goodness to them in their return from captivity. But God's forgiving love continues. He punishes the wrong-doers, but consoles the righteous. An added feature, however, is evident: God not only blesses his own covenant people, but extends his mercy to the Gentiles. Isaiah had already hinted at this. Now it becomes a prominent theme. The Messiah who is a covenant for Israel will become a light for the Gentiles. In this, Israel has a significant part to play.

Aspects of Christ recalled with a new emphasis

From our viewpoint, however, these final oracles are intriguing. They recall aspects of Christ already foretold in the earlier chapters and stress these truths freshly in a historical context of joy, as Israel returns from exile and settles in the homeland. The features we have already seen recur again.

The coming of Christ

The coming of Christ is evident with yet more specific detail as to its ultimate fulfilment:

'Arise shine, for your light has come,
  and the glory of the Lord rises upon you.
See, darkness covers the earth
  and thick darkness is over the peoples,
but the Lord rises upon you
  and his glory appears over you.
Nations will come to your light,
  and kings to the brightness of your dawn...

Then you will look and be radiant,
  your heart will throb and swell with joy;
the wealth on the seas will be brought to you,
  to you the riches of the nations will come.
Herds of camels will cover your land,
  young camels of Midian and Ephah.
And all from Sheba will come,
  bearing gold and incense
  and proclaiming the praise of the Lord'

(Isa. 60:1-3, 5-6).

Earlier the Messiah's coming, as light shattering the darkness, was directed primarily to the regions of Zebulun and Naphtali, even though Galilee of the Gentiles was included (Isa. 9:1). Now the parameters of his coming are widened. Nations and kings come, sons and daughters travel from a distance, herds of camels track from Midian and Ephah, eastern gold and incense are brought from Sheba in South Arabia, trading ships bear cargoes from western Tarshish, foreigners rebuild Zion's walls and alien kings serve God's people. All regions are affected by the light of Christ's coming. Foreign nations are drawn within the ambit of Israel and Judah. Gentiles bless the people of God and share in the blessings of the covenant God of Israel.

This process, ultimately fulfilled in Jesus, had already been anticipated in Solomon. The visit of the Queen of Sheba was unforgettable. Her amazement was complete. Psalm 72 speaks in a vivid way of his greater successor:

'The kings of Tarshish and of distant shores
  will bring tribute to him;
the kings of Sheba and Seba
  will present him gifts.
All kings will bow down to him
  and all nations will serve him'

(Ps. 72:10-11).

With Jesus' coming, the oracle is complete. Matthew, conscious of the fulfilment of Scripture in Christ, recalls the visit of the Magi from the east. They seek a king and bear regal gifts — gold, incense, myrrh to honour his birth (Matt. 2:1-11). John, sensitive to the time of Messiah's death, records how Greeks sought Jesus and how Jesus regarded this as the divine signal for his final glorification in death: 'The hour has come for the Son of Man to be glorified' (John 12:23). Both at the outset and close of Jesus' ministry east and west come to him — an indication that, in the event, his sons and daughters will be from every tribe, tongue and nation under heaven. A greater than Solomon had come and the Gentiles would share in his glory.

The anointing of the Spirit

The kingdom of Christ is represented as the daughter of Zion married to her Saviour, a city no longer deserted but renamed Hephzibah, 'my delight in her', and Beulah, 'married'. It is a kingdom established by a bridegroom who is the Spirit-filled Messiah:

> 'The Spirit of the Sovereign Lord is on me,
>   because the Lord has anointed me
>   to preach good news to the poor.
> He has sent me to bind up the broken-hearted,
>   to proclaim freedom for the captives
>   and release from darkness for the prisoners,
> to proclaim the year of the Lord's favour
>   and the day of vengeance of our God,
> to comfort all who mourn,
>   and provide for those who grieve in Zion '
>
> (Isa. 61:1-3).

Isaiah had already announced the Messiah's kingdom resulting from the Spirit's anointing (Isa. 11:1-5). There, the emphasis was on the way in which the Spirit would equip the Messiah for his work — with wisdom, understanding, counsel, power, knowledge and the fear of the Lord. But even then, God had promised that this kingdom would extend beyond Israel. The earth would be full of the knowledge of the Lord as the waters cover the sea. The root of Jesse would stand as a banner for the nations. They would rally to him (Isa. 11:9-10).

In this later oracle, the Spirit's anointing is again prominent. Here, the stress is on the nature of the Messiah's work: preaching good news to the poor, healing the broken-hearted, liberating the enslaved, announcing God's victory (Isa. 61:1-3). The relevance of this kingdom for the Gentiles receives even greater prominence now. Aliens shepherd the flocks of God's people and foreigners work their vineyards. Israel feeds on the wealth of nations, is known among the nations and acknowledged by them as blessed of God. The sovereign Lord makes their righteousness and praise spring up before all nations. The nations see Israel's righteousness; all kings view her glory. This comes about through God's Messiah. The Messiah is now the Bridegroom of his people. Israel is his bride. Israel is happy, loved and fruitful — a germinating seed, a growing plant, a royal diadem. The banner for the nations makes Jerusalem the praise of the earth (Isa. 61:5 - 62:7). The marriage has an issue beyond the confines of God's ancient covenant people. The kingdom of the Messiah is worldwide. Of that kingdom there is no end.

Luke points to Jesus as the Spirit-filled Messiah. Of all the Gospel writers, he stresses most clearly the fulfilment of this prophecy. Jesus is anointed by the Spirit in his baptism, is led full of the Spirit to temptation in the desert, returns in the power of the Spirit to his homeland of Galilee where, reading of the anointing of the Spirit from the scroll of Isaiah in his local synagogue in Nazareth, he unashamedly applies that scripture to himself: 'Today this scripture is fulfilled in your hearing' (Luke 4:21).

This emphasis on the inclusion of the Gentiles is a feature throughout Luke's Gospel. We see it from the very outset. Simeon announces Jesus' birth as a saving light for the Gentiles and a glory to God's people Israel (Luke 2:30-32; cf. Isa. 42:6; 49:6). John the Baptist prepares a way for the Lord. This ultimately means that all mankind see God's salvation (Luke 3:6; cf. Isa. 40:3-5). Luke traces Jesus' line of priestly descent beyond Abraham to Adam (Luke 3:38). When Jesus' townsfolk question his claim in the synagogue in Nazareth, Luke recalls Jesus' commendation of the widow of Zarephath in the region of Sidon and Naaman the Syrian (Luke 4:24-27). Clearly, Luke sees Jesus not only as Isaiah's Spirit-filled Messiah, but as the light of the Gentiles, the banner of the nations. Luke's portrayal of Jesus fulfils this later oracle of Isaiah to perfection.

Comfort for all mankind

The salvation of Christ offers the same rich comfort that Isaiah had earlier mentioned. A way will be prepared and a consolation provided.

'And it will be said:

"Build up, build up, prepare the road!
    Remove the obstacles out of the way of my people."

For this is what the high and lofty One says—
　he who lives for ever, whose name is holy:
"I live in a high and holy place,
　but also with him who is contrite and lowly in spirit,
to revive the spirit of the lowly
　and to revive the heart of the contrite...
Peace, peace, to those far and near,"
　says the Lord. "And I will heal them."
But the wicked are like the tossing sea,
　which cannot rest,
　whose waves cast up mire and mud.
"There is no peace," says my God, "for the wicked"'
(Isa. 57:14-15, 19-21).

'For this is what the Lord says:

"I will extend peace to her like a river,
　and the wealth of nations like a flooding stream;
you will nurse and be carried on her arm
　and dandled on her knees.
As a mother comforts her child,
　so will I comfort you;
　and you will be comforted over Jerusalem"'
(Isa. 66:12-13).

Isaiah's earlier word of comfort had been specifically addressed to Judah. A host of prophetic voices were summoned by God to bring consolation to Jerusalem, to speak to the very heart of God's people and remind them that the Messiah, as Prophet, Priest and King, would speak God's Word to them, tenderly deal with their plight and sovereignly provide a way of escape for them. God himself would lead them from captivity (Isa. 40:1-11).

Yet, even then, those outside Judah would see something of God's greatness. The divine disclosure, while for Judah's benefit, would ultimately affect all mankind:

'And the glory of the Lord will be revealed,
　and all mankind together will see it.
For the mouth of the Lord has spoken'
(Isa. 40:5).

For all mankind, not only Judah, are fallen and prone to sin. The need of God's comfort is universal: 'All men are like grass, and all their glory is like the flowers of the field' (Isa. 40:6).

Isaiah's later oracle stresses this universality. A road is to be built up and prepared. Obstacles are to be removed for God's people. But God's blessing is with those lowly in spirit and contrite in heart. Indeed, God's peace is for those far and near. That peace enlarges like a broad, flowing river. The wealth of nations will come to God's people. Involvement of the Gentiles, even at this level, is in view (Isa. 57:14-15,19; 66:12). The distinction now is as much between the contrite and the wicked as between Judah and her enemies. These truths have general import and anticipate the inclusion within God's kingdom and under Messiah's rule not only of the repentant of Judah, but also that of the nations. The broad, flowing river of God's grace will extend even to the Gentiles.

This finds pointed fulfilment in the ministry of Jesus. The covenant blessings of Christ's kingdom, the principles of the new law he promulgates, are for those poor in spirit, mournful in heart, meek in attitude, hungry and thirsty for righteousness — in a word for those who, recognizing their sin, become lowly and contrite in spirit, broken before God (Matt. 5:1-6). Theirs is the kingdom of heaven. God dwells with such people, regardless of race or nation. The comfort which Christ promises his disciples of a heavenly home with many rooms for them, the peace he bequeaths, which is unique and lasting, unlike the peace the world gives, comes only through himself and is open to all men. 'Whoever has my commands and obeys them, he is the one who loves me. He who loves me will be loved by my Father and I too will love him and show myself to him' (John 14:21). Peter learnt this lesson well from Christ when he proclaimed a gospel of peace for those both near and far: 'The promise is for you and your children and for all who are far off — for all whom the Lord our God will call' (Acts 2:39). The river of God's consoling grace finds completion in Jesus, the way, the truth and the life, and it is a grace open to Gentile as well as to Jew.

A sovereign Saviour and a tender Servant

The work of Christ is, again, both that of a sovereign Son defeating his enemies and a tender Servant helping his friends:

'Who is this coming from Edom,
    from Bozrah, with his garments stained crimson?
Who is this, robed in splendour,
    striding forward in the greatness of his strength?
"It is I, speaking in righteousness,
    mighty to save."
Why are your garments red,

like those of one treading the winepress?
"I have trodden the winepress alone;
   from the nations no one was with me.
I trampled them in my anger
   and trod them down in my wrath;
their blood spattered my garments,
   and I stained all my clothing.
For the day of vengeance was in my heart,
   and the year of my redemption has come"'

(Isa. 63:1-4).

'In all their distress he too was distressed,
   and the angel of his presence saved them.
In his love and mercy he redeemed them;
   he lifted them up and carried them
   all the days of old'

(Isa. 63:9).

Edom was an age-old enemy of Israel. The Edomites were the descendants of Esau. The name 'Edom', meaning 'red', could refer to the red stew traded for Esau's birthright or to the Red Sea area occupied by the Edomites in the south-eastern corner of Palestine. The Edomites were a constant thorn in Israel's side. They blocked Israel's passage at the time of the Exodus. In Jehoshaphat's reign they joined the Ammonites and Moabites in raiding Judah. In Isaiah's own day, during the attack by Pekin and Rezin, they invaded Judah and carried off captives. When Judah eventually fell, they rejoiced and encouraged her enemies to raze Jerusalem to the ground. The prophets foretold Edom's judgement because of this hatred (Jer. 49:7-22; Ezek. 25:12-14; Joel 3:19; Amos 9:12). Here, Isaiah depicts the Messiah returning from Edom's capital Bozrah, his garments stained with Edomite blood. He alone has trodden the winepress of the fury of God and destroyed Israel's enemy. His garments are 'red' with Edom's blood.

The Messiah, who powerfully destroys his enemies, does so to protect and show kindness to his friends. His warlike activities and glorious triumph are for his people's benefit. They are blessed under his rule. He has done many good things for the house of Israel. His compassion comes from his covenant love: 'Surely they are my people, sons who will not be false to me' (Isa. 63:8). In that setting, the Messiah relates to them as a Saviour carrying out his sovereign work, a tender Servant identifying with his people in their distresses, saving them from desolation, redeeming them from slavery, lifting them up and carrying them off from captivity.

John sees the ultimate fulfilment of all this in his vision on Patmos (Rev. 19:11-21). Heaven stands open and a white horse appears. But it is the rider on that horse who fills John's gaze. He is the same figure as John saw in his first vision standing in majesty among the churches — the Son of Man, his eyes blazing like fire, his head crowned with many crowns. His name is Faithful and True, the Word of God. At the same time, there is a secrecy about his name — the rider alone knows the depths of his own true identity. His robe catches John's eye. It is dipped in blood. That stands in stark contrast with the host of riders on white horses who follow their leader. They are dressed in fine linen, white and clean. It is as though his blood-stained robe makes theirs clean. A sword comes from his mouth which strikes down the nations. The leader on the white horse brings to pass the words of the psalmist: 'He will rule them with an iron sceptre' (Rev. 19:15; cf. Ps. 2:9). The rider fulfils the promise of the prophets. 'He treads the winepress of the fury of the wrath of God Almighty' (Rev. 19:15). The name on his robe and thigh, above all, catches John's attention: King of Kings and Lord of Lords. These words make sense of the subsequent victory of the rider, the defeat of the beast and the false prophet, the total destruction of his enemies.

What Isaiah hints at, John sees fully. The prophet's servant avenger routs his enemies for his people's good. The seer's triumphant rider is Lord of all kings and presides over all nations. The host in white linen are there, not because of ancient racial rights, but because of fulfilled covenant promises. The Lamb whom John sees sitting on the throne is the Lamb slain before the foundation of the earth. The ram who protects the flock is the lamb who has been sacrificed for them. The sheep comprise all peoples and nations, for there are others not of this fold whom the Messiah must bring into the flock. He does this because he is both a covenant for his people and a light to the Gentiles. The Gentiles share in the triumphant saving blessings of the covenant. Christ accomplishes this as Lord of all nations. He is King of Kings and Lord of Lords.

The problem of sin and the grace of God

The gospel of Christ exhibits the same hopelessness of man in sin and free gift of God's forgiveness in mercy:

> 'All of us have become like one who is unclean,
>   and all our righteous acts are like filthy rags;
> we all shrivel up like a leaf,
>   and like the wind our sins sweep us away'

(Isa. 64:6).

'I revealed myself to those who did not ask for me;
   I was found by those who did not seek me.
To a nation that did not call on my name,
   I said, "Here am I, here am I"'

                                                    (Isa. 65:1).

At the end of the day, Isaiah realized that God's people were under his judgement because of sin. In spite of the awesome things that God had done for Israel, they continued to sin against God. God was rightly angry. This behaviour offended his justice. God comes to the help of those who do right and remember his ways. But Israel had not done that.

The problem of sin was fearful. It was universal. They were all like unclean lepers. It was endemic. All their righteous acts were like rotten rags. It was devastating. It drained life and vitality from them. There was no substance to their existence. They were like shrivelled autumn leaves blown away by winter winds. Their situation was hopeless. 'How then can we be saved?' cried the prophet (Isa. 64:5).

Isaiah finds the answer in the grace of God, the same free gift of God's forgiveness he had proclaimed in an earlier oracle (Isa. 55). They must come to God's waters and drink. There they could procure wine and milk without money and without price. Here the image of grapes persists. As when some juice is left in an indifferent bunch of grapes and men say, 'Don't destroy it, there is yet some good in it,' so God will not destroy all his people. He will bring out a remnant, descendants of Jacob and Judah, whom he will bless with abundance of flocks and herds (Isa. 65:8-10).

The striking feature about God's actions, however, is that this free gift of grace will be offered to the Gentiles. As in the earlier oracle Isaiah prophesied unknown nations seeking the Messiah, so now the method of how that will come about is detailed:

'I revealed myself to those who did not ask for me;
   I was found by those who did not seek me.
To a nation that did not call on my name,
   I said, "Here am I, here am I"'

                                                    (Isa. 65:1).

Again the answer lies in the grace of God. The very method lies in that grace too. Not only the gospel of forgiveness, but the disclosure of that gospel is gratuitous. God's revelation to the Gentiles arises from his free covenant love. The Messiah who is a light to the Gentiles is sent by God for that very purpose.

Paul highlights these truths in his letter to the Romans. All mankind stands hopeless at the bar of God's justice. The heathen is condemned, for he sins against the invisible God, visibly evident in creation. The Greek shares his grief. He infringes the law of God written on his conscience. The Jew is equally guilty. He commands others to keep God's law yet breaks it himself. All are guilty, Jew and Gentile alike — silent, inexcusable before the eternal Judge. The reason is the same as that given by Isaiah: the universal and devastating nature of sin. All have sinned and fallen short of the glory of God. As Isaiah taught through the imagery of shrivelled leaves, so Paul cites prophet and psalmist to stress the effects of sin in man's mind, actions, speech, intention and attitude — a total depravity, an impossible plight (Rom. 1:18 - 3:20).

Paul's answer is in the gospel of Christ, the Messiah. Christ provides a gift of righteousness, a divine disclosure apart from law to which both Law and Prophets testify (Rom. 3:21). More than that, God provides through Christ a way of including the Gentiles in this gospel of grace. The picture of the olive tree replaces that of the vine. Branches are broken off the natural olive tree so that the Gentiles, a wild olive shoot, might be grafted in and thus enjoy the blessings of life and fruitfulness. But there must be no boasting, either by Jew nor Gentile. It is all of grace. The methodology of that grace Paul traces to Scripture — first Moses, then Isaiah (Rom. 10:19-21):

'Again I ask: Did Israel not understand? First, Moses says,

"I will make you envious by those who are not a nation;
    I will make you angry by a nation that has no understanding."

'And Isaiah boldly says,
"I was found by those who did not seek me;
    I revealed myself to those who did not ask for me."

'But concerning Israel he says,
"All day long I have held out my hands
    to a disobedient and obstinate people"'
                        (Rom. 10:19-21; cf. Deut. 32:21; Isa. 65:1,2).

Isaiah, in prospect, forecasts the solution of sin in the free gift of righteousness through a revealed Messiah — a covenant for Israel, a light for the Gentiles. Paul, in retrospect, affirms the truth of this. It is all of the divine purpose, the gospel of God's grace in Christ the Messiah. The blessing of Abraham comes to Gentiles through Jesus

Christ, and it comes to them in the same way and on the same gratuitous terms as to Jews — by faith (Gal. 3:14).

Christ in Isaiah

The only noticeable omission, overtly at least, in chapters 56-66 is that of Christ's death. Christ's death, of course, is implicit in the sympathetic Servant who identifies with his people. But the note of victory so predominates these closing chapters that the Messiah's death is not explicitly mentioned. In this regard, Isaiah 53 stands in 'splendid isolation', moulding the whole of Old Testament expectation in the direction of a Servant who not only suffers but dies for his people. The omission is natural in these final oracles for death itself, as it were, has been swallowed up in victory.

Christ, however, is there, just as prominent in position, awe-inspiring in vision and glorious in triumph as in all Isaiah. The more we think of it, the more evident it is that Christ is in all Scripture — Law, Prophets and Writings. He is throughout the prophecy: the ultimate fulfilment of every oracle, the motive of each God-breathed word, the final issue of the prophet's declarations, both in the history of his own lifetime and in the prediction of later events.

As we turn to the New Testament, we also see Isaiah in Christ's mind. We readily understand the comment that, while 'Servant' was not one of the titles by which Jesus described himself, or one which many attributed to him, yet it played so prominent a part in his thinking and motivation that the word might almost seem at times to tremble on Jesus' lips. 'For even the Son of Man did not come to be served, but to serve, and to give his life as a ransom for many' (Mark 10:45; cf. Isa. 53:12).

Augustine was right. The New is in the Old concealed; the Old is in the New revealed. There is no clearer illustration of this than the Christ of Isaiah. Our hearts begin to burn within us, our minds are cleared of confusion, our wills are challenged to obedience by the Christ of Isaiah, who is both Saviour and Lord. Like the Ethiopian treasurer, with great excitement and eagerness, we are moved to follow and serve him. We know Christ better, too, through this exercise. It is as though he opens the Scriptures to us, Scriptures which meant so much to him as he exercised his ministry on earth. We peer with reverence into his mind and see the satisfaction he had in fulfilling his Father's will. This glorifies Christ and does us inestimable good. It moves us to find him as Saviour and to serve him as Lord. May that ever be the case!

Behold my Servant! See him rise
Exalted in my might!
Him have I chosen, and in him
I place supreme delight.

On him, in rich effusion pour'd,
My Spirit shall descend;
My truths and judgements he shall show
To earth's remotest end.

Gentle and still shall be his voice,
No threats from him proceed;
The smoking flax he shall not quench,
Nor break the bruised reed.

The feeble spark to flames he'll raise;
The weak will not despise;
Judgement he shall bring forth to truth,
And make the fallen rise.

The progress of his zeal and pow'r
Shall never know decline,
Till foreign lands and distant isles
Receive the law divine.

He who erected heaven's bright arch,
And bade the planets roll,
Who peopled all the climes of earth,
And form'd the human soul,

Thus saith the Lord, 'Thee have I rais'd,
My Prophet thee install;
In right I've rais'd thee, and in strength
I'll succour whom I call.

I will establish with the lands
A covenant in thee,
To give the Gentile nations light;
And set the pris'ners free.'

(Isa. 42. Scottish Paraphrases)